Avgusta Udart

Easy Recorder Lessons
for Kids

VIDEO AND AUDIO

Beginner Recorder
for Children and Teens with 60 Songs.
First Book Step by Step

Watch me play the piano along with learning

Messages about typos, errors, inaccuracies and suggestions for improving the quality are gratefully received at:
avgustaudartseva@gmail.com

CONTENTS

Chapter 1

About recorder

Chapter 2

Theory & Practice

Chapter 3

About recorder

Foreword

If you've never played a wind instrument and would like to try, this book is just what you need! It will help you learn how to play the recorder. Don't worry if you don't know much yet about music and notes. Here you will find everything you need to know about how to read music and also how to play an instrument!

The recorder is easy to learn. As you learn to play it, you will also be learning to breathe right. This can become a fascinating new experience that also has great health benefits!

In this book you will learn all the basics of playing the recorder. You will also learn to play simple well-known tunes starting with the very first days of training!

You can do it! Good luck!

Avgusta Udartseva

Recorder background

The first mention of the recorder appears in the 9th century (Medieval era). The recorder of those times, of course, differed from the modern one, but it was already the recorder and not a fife.

In the 14th century the recorder was the most important instrument that was used to accompany singing. The sound of the instrument was not loud and very melodious. It is generally believed that itinerant musicians greatly contributed to its widespread use. The first sheet music for the recorder appears in the 16th century.

Johann Sebastian Bach
1685 – 1750

Antonio Vivaldi
1678 – 1741

Georg Friedrich Handel
1685 – 1759

In the 17th century the recorder was fully adapted to be used as a solo instrument. A collection of pieces for the recorder appeared authored by the Dutch composer Jacob Van Eyck.

Later, such famous composers as Johann Sebastian Bach, George F. Handel, and Antonio Vivaldi all wrote music for the recorder. The instrument sounded remarkably well in chamber music ensembles intended for small groups of listeners. In this form, the recorder as a professional instrument existed until the late 18th century and even into the early 19th century. At that point the recorder moved on to become an instrument for amateur musicians making way on the concert stage for modern flute (sometimes called the transverse flute, because it is played in a position parallel to the floor). The flute is what you usually see today in symphony orchestras.

A renaissance of the recorder took place at the end of the 19th century. There was a renewed interest in the baroque instruments as well as in the music of the time period of Bach and Handel. The time was ripe for the return of the recorder back to limelight.

Best modern recorder virtuosos

You should know at least a few of the best recorder virtuosos. Among them are the German recorder player Maurice Steger, the Czech Jiří Stivín and the Danish Michala Petri. They all play a wide variety of recorder music.

Recorder family

There are six most common types of recorders that you will meet. Starting from the smallest to the largest they are: sopranino, soprano, alto, tenor, bass and great bass.

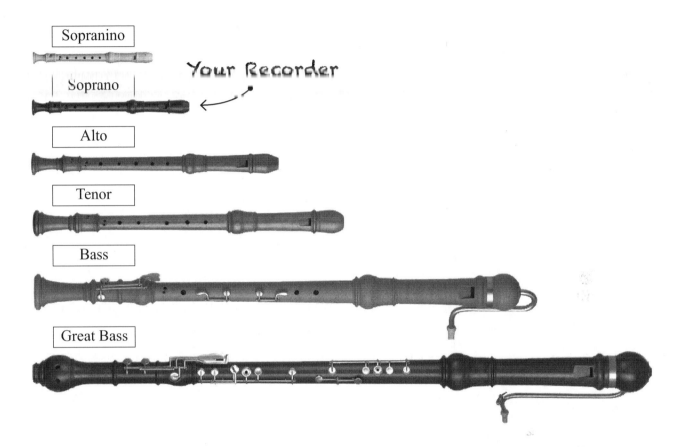

Depending on the size of the instrument it sounds higher or lower, for example the smallest instrument sounds very high and the largest instrument sounds very low. This allows the recorder ensemble to play almost any kind of music.

Each instrument has its own scale. What does this mean? If you played the C note on the piano, it would match the C of the Soprano (or Descant) recorder. The treble recorder is played in the F scale. That means that the C of the treble recorder will not match the C note on the piano.

SOPRANINO 9 inches long, smallest in size and has the highest pitch (it is tuned in the F key).

SOPRANO This is the most commonly played instrument (second from top in the picture), also called the Descant. This is the instrument we will talk about in this book. The soprano is about 12.5 inches long and is a leading musical instrument. The "C" note of this recorder is the same as the "C" note on the piano (it has a C scale), but the notes actually sound 8 sounds (one octave) higher than written

ALTO It is about 18.5 inches long and is the main instrument of the whole family. Just like the sopranino, it is tuned in the F key.

TENOR It is about 25½ inches long. The notes are written as they sound. This instrument is often used in ensemble playing. Like the soprano recorder, the tenor is tuned in the key of C.

BASS It has a length of about 36 inches. It is primarily an ensemble instrument. The notes are written as they sound. Like alto and sopranino recorder, the bass recorder sounds in the key of F.

GREAT BASS It is about 49 inches long, has a wider body than the bass recorder and has a larger, richer tone. It sounds in the key of C just like the soprano and tenor recorders.

Types of recorder material

Recorders can be made of wood, plastic or a combination of the two.

Wood recorders. Earlier recorders were made exclusively of wood. Modern recorders can be made of boxwood, sapele (African mahogany), fruit trees such as plum, pear, apple and olive, as well as of oak and maple. Each type of wood gives the instrument a different tone, but in general the sound of the wooden recorder can be characterized as soft, lively and expressive. A disadvantage of wood recorders is the need for careful maintenance. You have to keep the wood from excessive humidity as well as maintain good instrument hygiene.

Plastic recorders. You will likely have a plastic recorder, which is an acceptable and even a welcome choice by many musicians. For the initial training a plastic recorder is preferable. It is more affordable and also more hygienic. It is also easier to handle and maintain. Its tone may appear a little more straightforward. Plastic instrument is more durable and it does not crack over time, as can happen with wood recorder. The plastic recorder has its own endless musical possibilities. In the end, everyone can choose an instrument according to his or her preference. The tone of the sound of the wood instrument is slightly more gentle and warm, despite the fact that it requires much more care than the plastic instrument does.

Combined recorders. This is a middle option between wood and plastic. These recorders have a wooden body, providing a warm, soft sound, and a plastic mouthpiece, which can be easily washed if necessary. These recorders cost more than the plastic ones, but they are far less expensive than wood recorders.

Conclusion. When choosing a recorder for yourself, first of all, you need to decide where you plan to play it. If you lead an active lifestyle, like hiking and traveling, want to always take your recorder with you, then feel free to buy a plastic one. It is more practical and will not be damaged by water, dirt, sunlight, and other elements. Keep in mind though that an inexpensive plastic recorder will sound more like a toy. If you want a good-sounding instrument and not just a toy, go for a quality plastic recorder. It will cost a little more, but you will not be disappointed. For concert performances the wood instrument is perfect since only wood can yield a beautiful and rich tone. When it comes to learning, it is best to start playing on a combined instrument. The wood base will produce quality tone that a beginner musician must get used to, while the plastic mouthpiece will not swell or lose its shape while you are learning to play correctly.

Any choice you make will be a good one! You can also start learning to play the recorder made of high quality ABS plastic – it's another great option!

Recorder maintenance

Wipe the instrument after each lesson, even if it was only for a short period of time. Why is instrument hygiene so important? When you exhale while playing, condensation forms and settles on the walls of the recorder. If it is not removed regularly, it will lead to a large build-up of bacteria inside the instrument, which may result in lessons no longer being useful. To avoid this, it is sufficient to wipe the recorder after each lesson with a fine cloth or to wash it under running water (Remember! A wood recorder should never be soaked in water). Clean the inside of the recorder with a special brush or a cleaning rod. For disinfection, you can treat the instrument completely (inside and outside) with a disinfectant solution or alcohol once a week.

 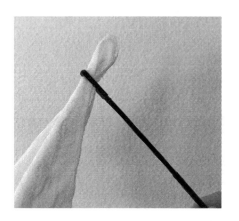 

Coat the joints with recorder cream when assembling your recorder. Wood recorders require extra care and lubrication. Never store a wood recorder in a place with high humidity or heat. Make sure the recorder is completely dry before storing it in its case. The recorder can also be cleaned using a toothbrush.

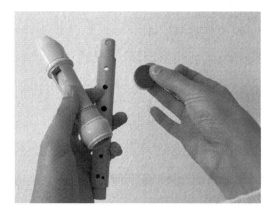 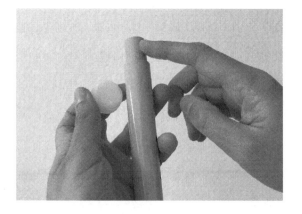

It is important to remember: the recorder is an individual musical instrument, so you should not let other people play your instrument!

Structure & Differences of recorders

As mentioned earlier, there are several types of recorders. In this book we will look in detail at the structure of the soprano or descant recorder.

A modern recorder consists of three sections: the head joint, the middle joint, and the foot joint. It is noteworthy that according to archaeological research the first version of the recorder consisted of one single section.

On a three-joint recorder, the foot joint can be rotated, offering the advantage of being able to adjust this section to reposition the tone hole so that it can be more easily reached by the little finger of the right hand.

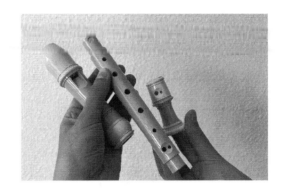

The recorder can also have two sections (only the top part can be detached).

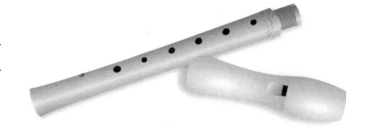

There are some one-section recorders that sometimes are used for educational purposes. However, since they have a plain tone and a toy-like feel, we recommend to avoid using it in the process of learning to play the instrument.

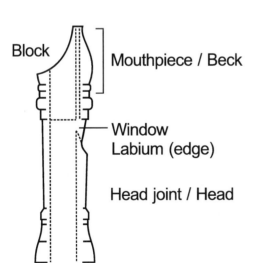

Block

Mouthpiece / Beck

Window
Labium (edge)

Head joint / Head

The sound of the recorder is born in the mouthpiece, which looks like a beak. Inside of the mouthpiece there is a wooden plug, which covers the air inlet leaving only a narrow slit.

 **Straight type.** Easy to play, gentle tone. Combines pleasantly.

 **Arched type.** Easier to control breath due to the degree of resistance felt when blowing. Brilliant tone with a degree of tension.

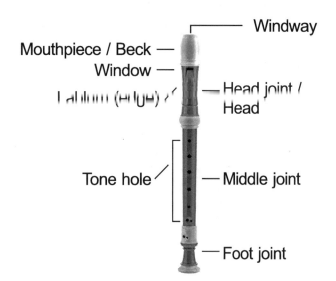

Windway

Mouthpiece / Beck —

Window —

Labium (High) ?

Head joint / Head

Tone hole

Middle joint

Foot joint

The pitch of the sound can be changed by covering the tone holes on the middle joint of the recorder.

There are a total of eight tone holes: seven on the front side and one on the back.

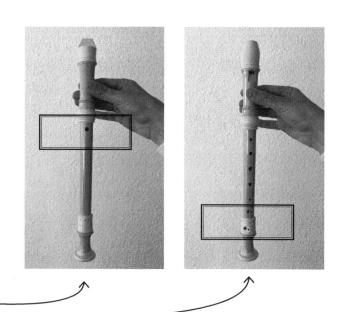

The back hole is called the "octave valve": By not closing it completely with your finger (just over half of the hole), you change the note you're playing by 8 sounds up (the note will sound an octave higher).

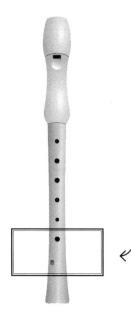

There are two double tone holes at the bottom of the recorder. They make it much easier for the performer to play half steps - all he has to do is to cover one of the two holes with his finger, and the needed note will sound.

On recorders with single tone holes, playing half steps clearly will be a bit more difficult - you need to cover half of the hole and any slight mistake leads to a change in pitch. However, this should not be viewed as a drawback since it allows you to have more control over the sound you're making.

What are the recorder differences?

Recorders are also classified by fingering systems.

The fingering system (German: Applikatur, Latin: applico "to apply, press") is the order in which the fingers are placed and alternated when playing a musical instrument.

There are two types of recorder fingering systems: **German** (Renaissance) and **Baroque** (English).

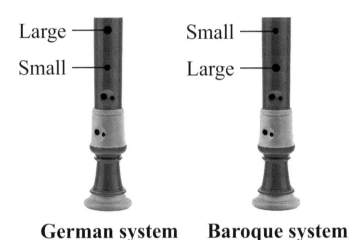

Large ——
Small ——

Small ——
Large ——

German system   **Baroque system**

The German fingering system is a little easier to learn, but the majority of the best professional instruments are made with the **Baroque fingering system.**

In the image provided you can notice that the difference between the two systems is only in the size of the two holes.

Which is better? German or Baroque fingering system? Double bottom tone holes or single holes?

This is a personal choice of the player. Professional musicians tend to choose the baroque system and single bottom holes as this combination allows for better sound control. Music school teachers adhere to the same position when recommending the instrument to their students. However, if you want to learn to play as quickly as possible and do not plan to play complicated pieces (at least at the start), get an instrument with **the German fingering** and double bottom holes. Should you ever decide to take up the recorder professionally in the future, it will not be too difficult to adjust to the other system and instrument layout.

Professional musicians usually have several different recorders at their disposal, but as a beginner it is best to get a soprano recorder in the key of C with the German fingering system.

Let's begin!

Before we get our hands on recorder, let's practice blowing properly. Raise the palm of your hand up to your face and imagine that you are blowing on a spoonful of hot oatmeal to cool it down. Don't blow hard, instead do it calmly and steadily.

Now imagine that you are blowing soap bubbles and blow gently without thrusting. Blowing softly with a steady flow of air is one of the most difficult but important techniques you will need to master as you learn to play the recorder.

Important: If you don't know what stomach breathing is, go to the mirror. Look at yourself. Inhale! Are your shoulders moving up? Then inhaling is no good. Breathe out. Try another breath using your stomach. If your stomach is rising while your shoulders and chest stay down, you've got it.

Assembling the instrument. The recorder usually consists of three parts: the head joint, which has a mouthpiece, the middle joint with finger holes, and the foot joint, which is shaped like a bell. Gently join the sections by twisting them together.

The bottom part should be turned so that the hole is slightly to the right when viewed from the player's side.

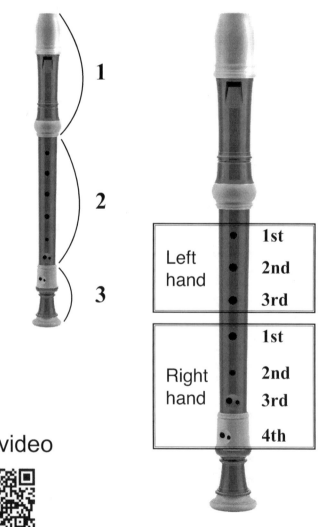

See video

Holding the recorder

It is best to learn to play the recorder while standing up but you can also do it while seated.

1. The left hand is placed at the top and the right hand is at the bottom. The back side with one hole should be facing your chest. The front side should be facing away from you.

Hold the recorder at about a 45-degree angle, as shown. This will direct the sound from the instrument directly toward the audience.

Place your right hand thumb (RT) on the back side of the recorder. Pick a spot that makes it easy to cover the opposite front holes with the 1st, 2nd, 3rd, and 4th fingers of your right hand, but do not cover them yet.

The performer's head, neck, and back should be in one straight line. Nothing should constrict the chest and the throat which should be relaxed.

2. Now bring the recorder close to your mouth. The tip of the recorder looks like a beak. Place the lower part of the beak on the middle of your lower lip and seal the upper part of the beak with your upper lip. Wrap your lips tightly around the tip of the whistle, but don't strain your lips! <u>Just the very tip of the mouthpiece should be kept between your lips.</u> Do this without effort, so that you can freely inhale and exhale air with your mouth.

3. Gently hold the mouthpiece between your lips and balance the recorder with your fingers. Do not cover any holes on the recorder yet! Learn to hold it.

Important: Do not bite the mouthpiece or let it touch your teeth.

Making your first sound

Blow into the recorder to get an idea of what it sounds like. You will need to blow gently. Breathe in through the corners of your lips with your lips slightly stretched out in a smile.

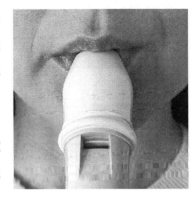

Each finger is assigned a number. The table chart shows you which holes you need to cover using which fingers to get the desired note.

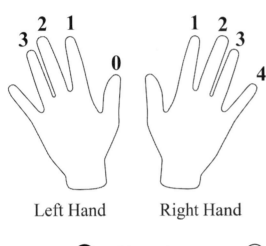

Left Hand   Right Hand

0 Left thumb
1 Left index finger
2 Left middle finger
3 Left ring finger

1 Right index finger
2 Right middle finger
3 Right ring finger
4 Right little finger

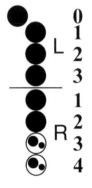

● Closed   ○ Open   ◐ Open 1/4*

The B note

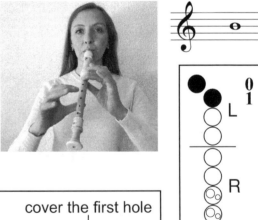

Cover the hole on the back with your left thumb and with your left index finger (1st finger) cover the top hole. Smoothly blow into the recorder as if saying (voicelessly) the syllable "too (tu)".

Pay attention to the use of the tongue in the process of playing recorder. When playing a note on the recorder, start and stop the sound with your tongue. Place your tongue on the palate behind your teeth. The sound should start and stop there.

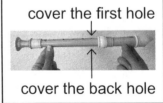

cover the first hole

cover the back hole

* The image is schematic. Close about 2/3 of the hole (a little more than half). See p. 60.

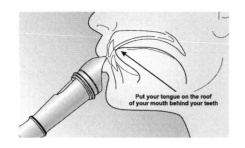

Put your tongue on the roof of your mouth behind your teeth

Important: Do not try to cover the holes with your fingertips.

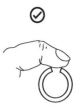

The A note

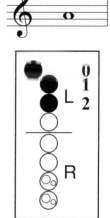

Using the 1st and 2nd fingers of your left hand, cover the top two holes on the front. The hole on the back that is covered with the thumb of your left hand remains covered as it for the B note.

The G note

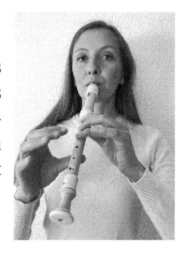
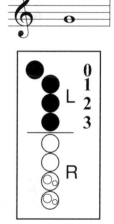

Now using the 1st, 2nd and 3rd fingers of your left hand close the top three holes on the front. The left 4th finger (little finger) does not cover the hole. The hole on the back covered by the thumb of the left hand remains covered.

The note F*

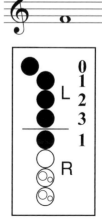

Now add the thumb and the 1st finger (index finger) of the right hand to get the note F. On the baroque system, it is a little more complicated (see the picture on the right).

* The German system. If the Baroque fingering system is used, see p. 44.

Finger movement

As you begin to lift or place more than one finger at a time, you may sense discomfort as the fingers may not want to move at once. Sometimes it's difficult to get to open two holes at the same time. There is nothing to worry! This is to be expected!

This skill comes gradually. With steady training for 10-15 minutes at a time the fingers will adapt and make different combinations easily, covering and opening the holes in the right order!

As you start, try not to lift your fingers too high above the holes. The best distance is the one that will allow you to place your finger back on the hole as quickly as possible (e.g., ¼ to ½ in.).

In the raised position, the finger should be exactly above its hole. If your finger moves away from this position, you'll have to look for the right hole every time.

Remember: if your finger moves away from its basic position, it will be a lot harder to cover the hole and get the note you want.

Breathing

Most of inhaling is done with your mouth through the corners of your lips. If you blow too hard, you will produce a harsh, unpleasant sound. Try blowing more gently to create a more melodious sound. Depending on the tune, the breath can be fast or slow, but always deep and using stomach muscles. That said, try not to draw in air using your chest. This will impede exhaling and make you lose all the air much quicker. It will also impair the sound of the recorder.

You should be able to produce a sustained note for about half a minute. If you cannot, you are blowing too hard.

It should be noted that there is an inextricable relationship between the note (sound) and the force with which you blow into the instrument. The higher the note, the more intensively you have to blow, and the lower the note, the softer you blow.

Tonguing

Close the gap between your lips with your tongue and quickly pull your tongue back and smoothly draw the sound from the recorder by saying the syllable "too (tu)". The "too (tu)" should be pronounced without using your voice. Some people pronounce the word "dah". In fact, it doesn't matter that much which syllable you pick. The important thing is to clearly articulate the letter "t." Why the letter "t"? This way the tongue blocks the gap between the lips, through where the air is flowing. The tongue should be pulled back to release the passage of air. Pull the tongue back - the air goes between the lips into the mouthpiece and the recorder gives sound. Place the tongue back between your lips - the air passage is blocked and the sound stops.

As you begin to learn, pay attention to the role of your tongue in your playing. Do not produce a sound simply by breathing air into the recorder. The tongue must shut off and open the flow of air. The sound should not stop on its own, as when you run out of air. You should stop the sound with your tongue.

Only when you see a curved line called a slur in the music connecting the notes, only then you do not separate notes from each other with your tongue or do it very gently. The melody will sound smooth and one sound will gently flow into another. But in this case, you should pay attention to finger articulation, so that the fingers are nimble, lifting up on time, otherwise the flow from one note to another will not be as precise.

No need to worry! Practice makes perfect! Practicing every day for 10-15 minutes you will be able to achieve great results!

Additional notes

1. Choose a recorder with the German fingering system.

2. Remember that the left hand is above the right hand and do not change the basic finger position set before playing.

3. Do not blow your cheeks while playing and do not bite the mouthpiece of the recorder with your teeth.

4. Use your tongue when playing individual notes (the word "Tu" or "Ta").

5. To produce a pleasant and clear tone:
- Relax your jaw.
- Use your tongue (too) to gently release a steady flow of air.
- Blow gently, not forcefully.

6. The higher the note, the harder you need to blow, and the lower the note, the softer the air flow. The lowest notes such as C, D and E require the most gentle blowing.

7. Take care of your instrument and wipe it down after every time you play it.

Moisture can be removed from the inside of the windway by covering the air stream window with your hand to muffle the sound and blowing hard into the instrument.

Chapter 2

ALL VIDEOS (Playlist)

All videos are also in the same playlist on YouTube:

or link:

cutt.ly/d8dN7YP

Messages about typos, errors, inaccuracies and suggestions for improving the quality are gratefully received at:
avgustaudartseva@gmail.com

Foreword

It is not enough to know how to play notes on the recorder, it is important to understand and read these notes. For this you will need to know the basics of music. In fact, they are not complicated at all. Once you learn the basic music theory you can then play not only the recorder, but any other instrument as well!

The world of music will open up to you in its entirety and you will be able to read tunes that you know and love!

Not only will your repertoire increase, but you'll also be able to record your own music if you should come up with a unique melody in a moment of inspiration.

There are different songs and melodies in this book. They are simple to play. You can practice using these songs and have fun learning all the basics of playing the recorder!

1. The Stave (Staff), Notes and Treble Clef

Music is written on a set of 5 lines called a *STAVE (STAFF*)*.

The TREBLE CLEF

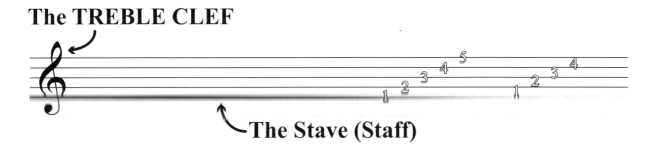

The Stave (Staff)

The two clefs that are basically used are the treble clef and the bass clef.

Music Notes are oval-shaped symbols that are placed on the lines, or in spaces between them. They represent musical sounds, called *PITCHES.*

The lines of the stave are numbered from bottom to top (1-5). The spaces between the lines are also numbered from bottom to top (1-4). If the notes appear higher on the stave, they sound higher in pitch. If the notes appear lower on the stave, they sound lower in pitch.

Music notes are named after the first seven letters of the alphabet:
A, B, C, D, E, F, G.

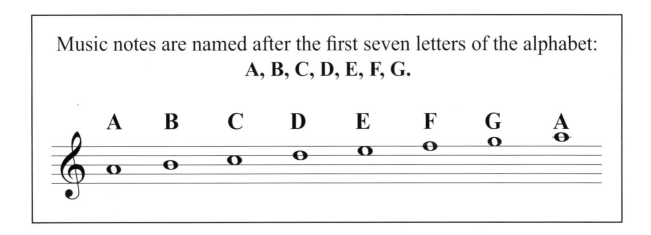

* Words "stave" and "staff" carry the same meaning referring to the five horizontal lines and four spaces between them used for music notation. The term "staff" is more common in the US while "stave" is more often used in Britain. In this book we use the term "stave".

In the treble stave, the names of the notes on the lines from bottom to top are **E, G, B, D, F.**

Notes on the Line

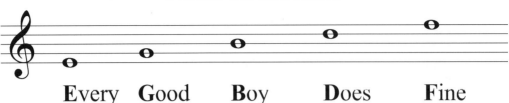

Every Good Boy Does Fine

Notes in the Spaces

The names of the notes in the spaces from bottom to top spell **FACE.**

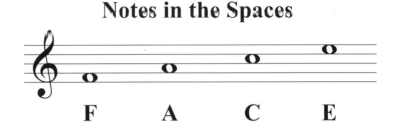

F A C E

Ledger lines are those little lines with notes on them that appear above or below a musical stave (staff):

The purpose of these lines is to extend the stave in both directions, up and down.

An *OCTAVE* is simply the distance between one note and that same note repeated in the next higher or lower register within the audible range.

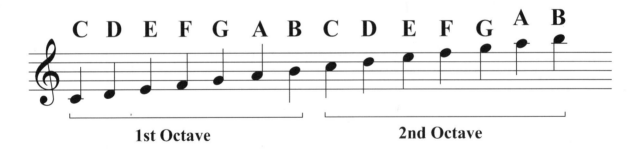

C D E F G A B C D E F G A B

1st Octave   2nd Octave

So then, we see that the notes are repeated (7 notes in total). The same note up an octave sounds exactly the same but higher.

Stems extend downward on the left side when the note appears on or above the 3rd line of the stave. Stems extend upward on the right side when the note appears below the 3rd line of the stave.

Stems Up   Stems Down

2. Note Values

While the placement of notes on the stave indicates the pitch, the duration of the note (how long the note is held down) is determined by the value of the note.

Whole note

A *WHOLE NOTE* is drawn as an open oval.

A whole note is equal to four counts (or beats). Count and clap the rhythm evenly (hands together for 4 beats). The beat numbers are written under the notes. Also, say "ta-ah-ah-ah" (in a continuous sound) and clap.

The whole note

𝗈 = 4 beats

(1 and 2 and 3 and 4 and)

The whole note

1 2 3 4

ta -ah -ah ah

Half notes

Two *HALF NOTES* equal the duration of one whole note.

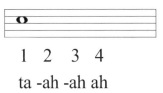

A half note is equal to two counts (or beats). Count and clap the rhythm evenly (holding your hands together for 2 beats). The beat numbers are written under the notes. Also, say "ta-ah" (in a continuous sound) and clap.

The half note

♩ = 2 beats

(1 and 2 and)

The half notes

1 2   3 4

ta -ah   ta -ah

Four *QUARTER NOTES* equal the duration of one whole note.

Quarter notes

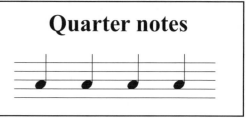

A quarter note is equal to one count (or beat). Count (1, 2, 3, 4) and clap the rhythm evenly (once per beat). The beat numbers are written under the notes. Also, say "ta" and clap.

The quarter notes

The quarter note

♩ = 1 beat (1 and)

1	2	3	4
ta	ta	ta	ta

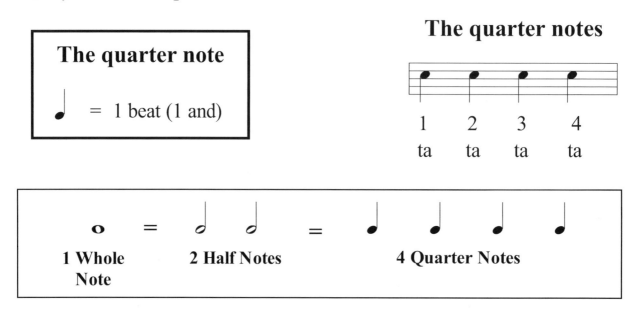

𝅝	=	𝅗𝅥 𝅗𝅥	=	♩ ♩ ♩ ♩
1 Whole Note		2 Half Notes		4 Quarter Notes

3. ⁴⁄₄ Time Signature, Measure, Bar Line

The *TIME SIGNATURE* appears at the beginning of the music after the clef sign. It contains two numbers, one above the other.

The upper number tells how many beats (or counts) are in each measure. In this case, 4.

The lower number indicates what type of note receives 1 beat. In this case, a quarter note.

The two numbers in the time signature are often replaced by the letter **C**.

$$\frac{4}{4} = \mathbf{C}$$

Music is divided into equal parts by *BAR LINES.* The area between the two bar lines is called a *MEASURE* or *BAR.*

A *DOUBLE BAR* is written at the end of a piece of music. It is made up of one thin and one thick line, with the thick line always on the outside.

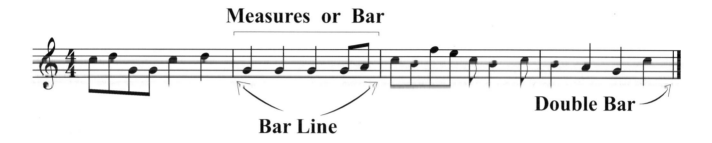

Note B

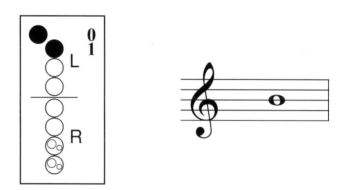

Play B

Clap the rhythm while counting

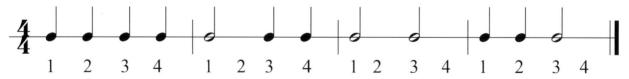

Now repeat this same rhythm using the B note

Music is not only made up of sounds, but also the silence between sounds. The duration of musical silence is determined by the value of the _REST._

A _WHOLE REST_ means to rest for a whole measure. It hangs down from the 4th line.	
An _HALF REST_ is equal to half of a whole rest. It sits on the 3rd line.	
A _QUARTER REST_ is equal to one quarter of a whole rest.	

In $\frac{4}{4}$ Time:

Quarter rests are equal to 1 beat.	1 2 3 4
Half rests are equal to 2 beats.	1 2 3 4
Whole rests are equal to 4 beats.	1 2 3 4

1 Quarter Note = 1 beat   1 Quarter Rest = 1 silent beat

Note A

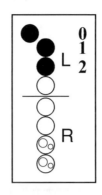

Play A

Tu   tu tu   tu   tu   tu tu   tu   tu   tu

1 2 3 4   1 2 3 4   1 2 3 4   1 2 3 4

Clap the rhythm while counting

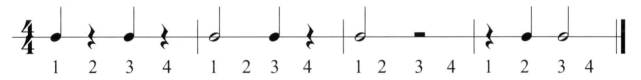

1 2 3 4   1 2 3 4   1 2 3 4   1 2 3 4

Now repeat this same rhythm using the A note

Tu   tu   tu   tu   tu   tu   tu

Eighth Note

When you add a flag to the stem of a quarter note, it becomes an *EIGHTH NOTE.*

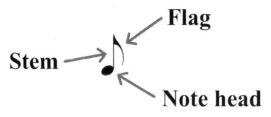

Two *EIGHTH NOTES* equal the duration of one quarter note.

Eighth notes

An eighth note is equal to one-half a count (or beat).

Count (1 and 2 and 3 and 4 and) and clap the rhythm evenly (once per beat and once per "and"). The beat numbers are written under the notes. Also, say "ti" and clap.

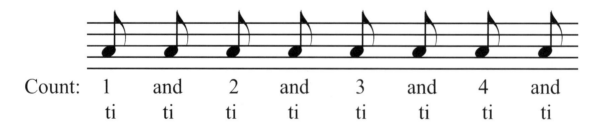

Count:	1	and	2	and	3	and	4	and
	ti	ti	ti	ti	ti	ti	ti	ti

Play

Two or more 8th notes are connected by a beam.

Beam

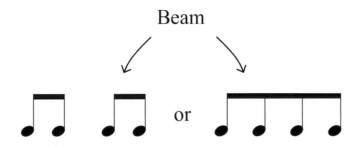

or

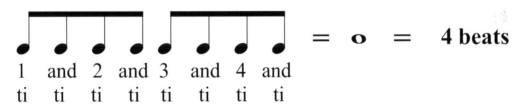

Two eighth notes equal 1 quarter note

♪ ♪ = ♩ = **1 beat**

1 and
ti ti

Four eighth notes equal 1 half note

= ♩ = **2 beats**

1 and 2 and
ti ti ti ti

Eight eighth notes equal 1 whole note

= o = **4 beats**

1 and 2 and 3 and 4 and
ti ti ti ti ti ti ti ti

Clap the rhythm while counting

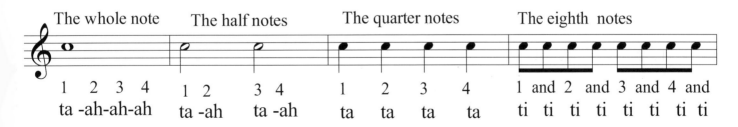

The whole note   The half notes   The quarter notes   The eighth notes

1 2 3 4   1 2   3 4   1   2   3   4   1 and 2 and 3 and 4 and
ta -ah-ah-ah   ta -ah   ta -ah   ta   ta   ta   ta   ti ti ti ti ti ti ti ti

Note G

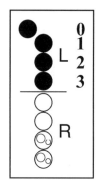

Play G

Tu	tu	tu	tu		tu	tu	tu		tu	tu		tu	tu	
1	2	3	4		1	2	3	4	1	2	3	4	1	2	3	4

Clap the rhythm while counting

1 & 2 & 3 & 4 & 1 & 2 & 3 & 4 & 1 & 2 & 3 & 4 & 1 & 2 & 3 & 4 &

Now you can easily play these songs. Write in note names before playing! ☺

Down By The Station

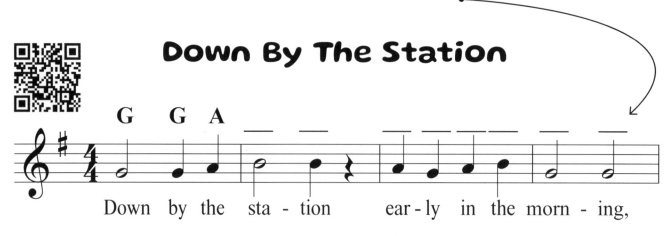

G G A ___ ___ ___ ___ ___

Down by the sta - tion   ear - ly in the morn - ing,

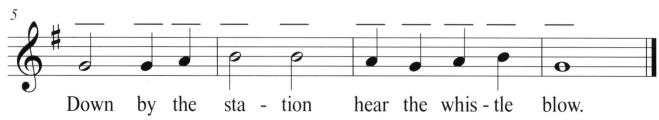

Down by the sta - tion   hear the whis - tle   blow.

Hot Cross Buns

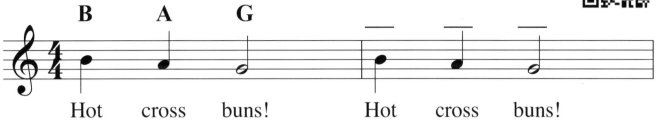

Hot cross buns! Hot cross buns!

One a pen - ny, two a pen - ny, hot cross buns!

Sleep, Baby Sleep

Sleep, ba - by sleep, The fath - er tends the sheep.

Moth - er shakes the dream-land tree, And down fall pleas - ant

dreams for thee, Sleep, ba - by, sleep.

Note C

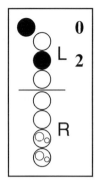

Play C

Tu				tu		tu		tu	tu	tu		tu	tu	tu	
1	2	3	4	1	2	3	4	1	2	3	4	1	& 2	3	4

Note D

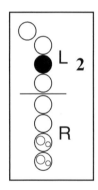

Play D

Tu		tu		tu		tu	tu	tu		tu	tu	tu	
1	2	3	4	1	2	3	4	1	2	3	4	1	2	3	4

Write in note names before playing! ☺

God Is So Good

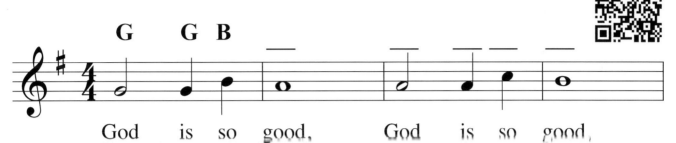

God   is   so   good,   God   is   so   good,

God   is   so   good,   He's   so   good   to   me.

Write down the rhythm of this song

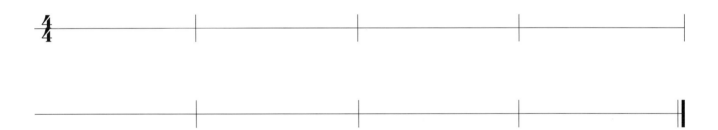

Remember

G   **A**   **B**   **C**   **D**

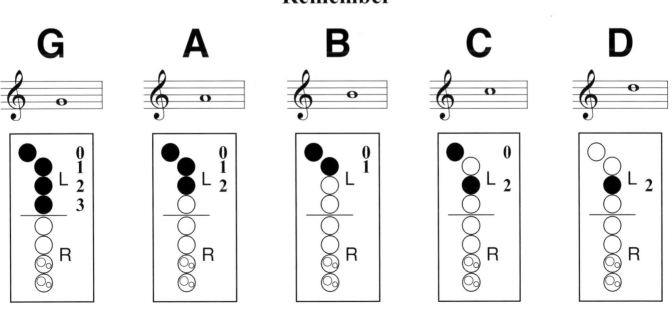

Ode To Joy

5. $\frac{2}{4}$ Time Signature

$\frac{2}{4}$ 2 means that there are 2 beats per measure;
4 means that the quarter note receives 1 beat.

$\frac{2}{4}$ and $\frac{4}{4}$ both have 4 as the bottom number, meaning a quarter note receives 1 beat. <u>The difference is that:</u> $\frac{2}{4}$ has 2 beats per measure while $\frac{4}{4}$ has 4.

Count: 1   2   1   2   1   2   1   2

A whole rest is used for a full measure of rest even if there are only 2 beats in each measure. When writing the music, a half rest and a whole note are never used in $\frac{2}{4}$ time.

Note E

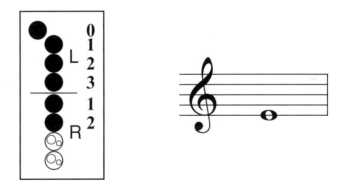

Play E

Tu   tu   tu tu   tu tu   tu   tu

1 & 2 & 1 & 2   &   1   & 2   &   1 & 2 &

6. ¾ Time Signature

¾   3 means that there are 3 beats per measure;
     4 means that the quarter note receives 1 beat.

Count: 1   2   3   1   2   3   1   2   3   1   2   3

A whole rest is used for a full measure of rest, even if there are only 3 beats in each measure. When writing the music, a half rest and a whole note are never used in ¾ time.

²⁄₄, ¾ and ⁴⁄₄ all have 4 as the bottom number, meaning the quarter note always receives 1 beat.

The difference is that: ²⁄₄ has 2 beats per measure; ¾ has 3 beats per measure; ⁴⁄₄ has 4 beats per measure.

Note F

Baroque fingering system

Play F

Tu   tu   tu   tu   tu   tu   tu tu   tu   tu   tu   tu   tu tu

Eighth rest ♪

An _EIGHTH REST_ ♪ is equal to half the value of a quarter rest 𝄾

Two 8th rests equal 1 quarter rest   ♪   ♪ = 𝄾
                                       1   and

Four 8th rests equal 1 half rest   ♪   ♪   ♪   ♪ = ▬
                                 1   and   2   and

Eight 8th rests equal 1 whole rest   ♪ ♪ ♪ ♪ ♪ ♪ ♪ ♪ = ▬
                                    1   and   2   and   3   and   4   and

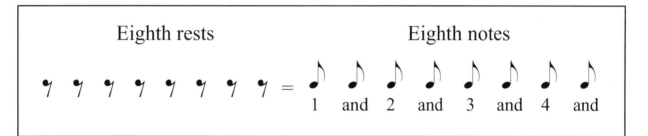

Eighth rests	Eighth notes
♪ ♪ ♪ ♪ ♪ ♪ ♪ ♪ =	♪ ♪ ♪ ♪ ♪ ♪ ♪ ♪
	1 and 2 and 3 and 4 and

Sixteenth note

 Sixteenth note = 1/4 beat

Clap the rhythm while counting

   1   & 2 & 3 & 4   &   1 & 2   & 3 & 4   &   1& 2& 3   &   4&   1& 2 & 3& 4&

An sixteenth rest is equal to half the value of a eighth rest

45

7. Dotted Note

A dot that is placed after the note to indicate a change in the duration of a note. The dot adds half of the value of the note to itself. For example, a dotted half note gets 3 beats - the value of a half note is 2, half of 2 is 1 so 2 + 1 = 3.

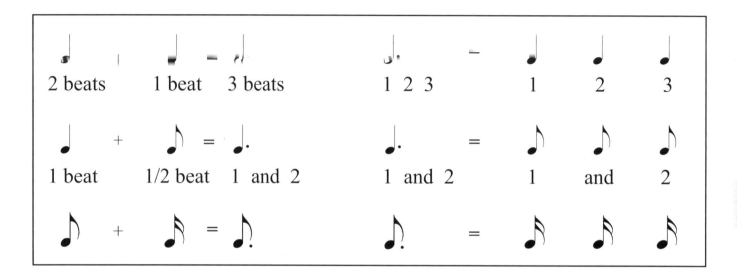

Clap the rhythm while counting

Dotted rhythms mix longer dotted notes with shorter undotted notes.

Clap the rhythm while counting

8. Sharp and Flat

The *SHARP* sign (♯) before a note raises the pitch of that note.

The *FLAT* sign (♭) before a note lowers the pitch of that note.

The note which is half a step higher than D is D sharp. The note which is half step lower than E is E flat.

ENHARMONIC NOTES - two notes that sound the same but are written differently (see p. 59).

9. Key Signatures

Usually certain sharps or flats are used throughout the piece. Writing in those sharps or flats every time they appear takes time and adds clutter. Instead, composers put them in a key signature, found just after the clef at the beginning of each stave. Key signatures tell us what notes are always sharp or flat in a given piece of music. Always read the sharps or flats in a key signature. Key signatures always have the sharps and flats listed in the same order. They always follow the same pattern.

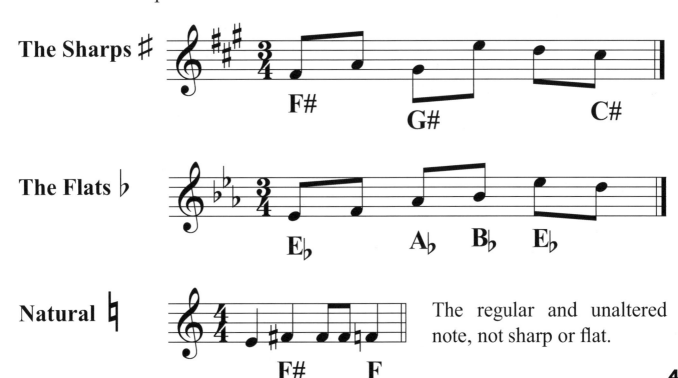

The Sharps ♯

F# G# C#

The Flats ♭

E♭ A♭ B♭ E♭

Natural ♮

F# F

The regular and unaltered note, not sharp or flat.

47

Note F#

Baroque fingering system

Note D

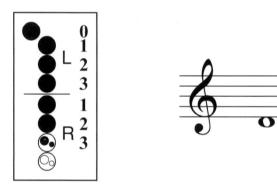

Play D

Play

Rain, Rain, Go Away

London Bridge Is Falling Down

10. ⁶⁄₈ Time Signature

⁶⁄₈ 6 means that there are 6 beats per measure;
8 means that the eight note receives 1 beat.

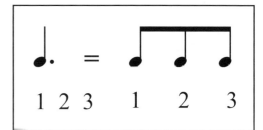

How to count in ⁶⁄₈ :

There are two ways to count a bar in ⁶⁄₈ time. This can seem confusing when you first encounter it, but as we'll see the difference is not as big as it first appears. You can either count it as:

*   6 eighth-note beats: 1, 2, 3, 4, 5, 6 = 1, 2, 3, 1, 2, 3
*   2 dotted-quarter-note beats: 1… 2…

Now you try:
Clap and say the beats:

Note C

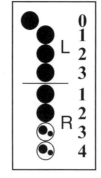

Play C

Play

Oh, Dear! What Can The Matter Be?

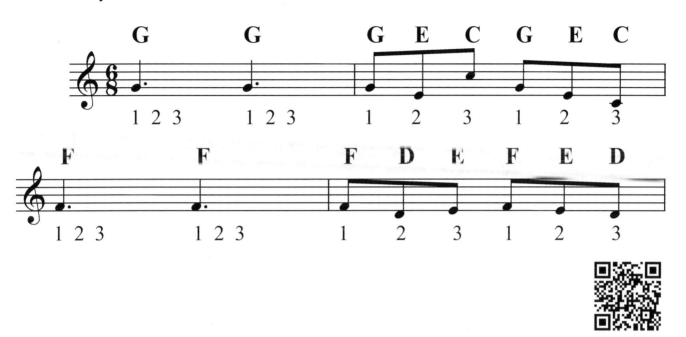

G	G	G E C	G E C
1 2 3	1 2 3	1 2 3	1 2 3

F	F	F D E	F E D
1 2 3	1 2 3	1 2 3	1 2 3

Humpty Dumpty

E G F A G A B C

Hump – ty Dump – ty sat on a wall.

E G F A G F E D

Hump – ty Dump – ty had a great fall.

11. Numbering of Measures

In this collection, the bars in each song are numbered. At the beginning of each next line of notes, a number is placed above the treble clef, which indicates the number of the measure. The numbering of measures in the first note line is not indicated.

Play

Fiddle-De-De

A _MEASURE_ is a unit of music. It is the space (area of music) between two bar lines. The time signature (the 2 numbers at the beginning of the melody) indicates how many beats are in a measure.

A first measure is called an _INCOMPLETE MEASURE_ when it does not contain the full number of beats as indicated by the time signature.

The notes in the first incomplete measure (the part of the counts found at the beginning of the music) are called the anacrusis, pick-up or upbeat.

An incomplete measure is a measure that is split or divided between the beginning and the end of the music.

Part of the measure is found at the beginning of the music. The remaining part of the measure is found at the end of the music.

The two "parts" must add up to one complete (full) measure.

$\frac{4}{4}$ = 4 beats per measure.

A-Tisket, A-Tasket

First incomplete measure

A - tis - ket, a - tas - ket a green and yel - low

bas - ket. I wrote a let - ter to my love and

on the way I dropped it, I dropped it, I

dropped it, and on the way I dropped it. A lit - tle boy he

picked it up and put it in his poc - ket.
1 2 3

Last incomplete measure

When a melody starts with an incomplete measure, it does not start with count #1!

Notes normally divide into two or four equal parts.

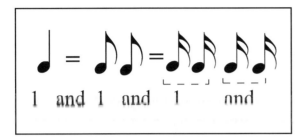

Triplets can be used to divide a note into three equal parts.

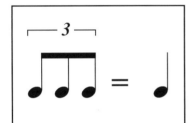

Triplets are indicated as three notes enclosed in square brackets and marked with the number 3.

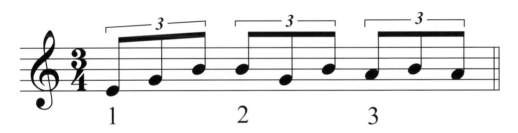

Quarter note = Two eighth notes = Three eighth-note triplets

Play

Wedding March

14. Articulation

ARTICULATION – the manner in which a note is performed.

A *TIE* joins two notes of the same pitch by a curved line over or under the notes. Each note joined by a tie is held for its full value but only the first note is played or sung. The tied note's value is added to the value of the first note.

Barcarolle

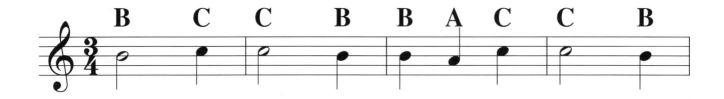

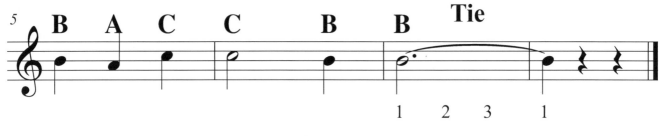

Clap the rhythm while counting

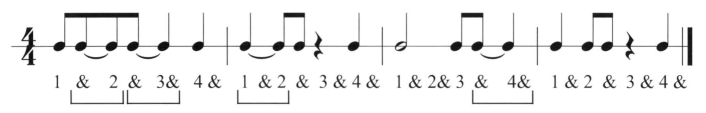

The tie should always be written on the opposite side of the note stems.

A *SLUR* smoothly connects two or more notes of different pitches by a curved line over or under the notes. There is no break in sound between pitches. This is also called playing or singing *LEGATO.*

Slur

Slur　　　　　　　　　　　　　　**Slur**

Note B♭

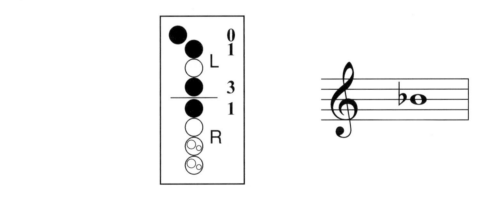

Play

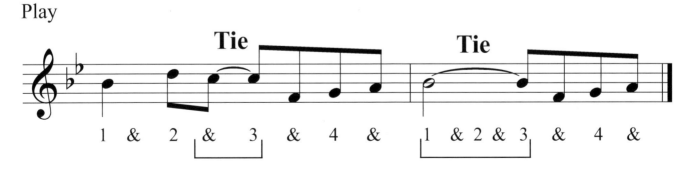

Repetition

Repeat signs

Enclose a passage that is to be played twice.

First and second endings

A repeated passage is to be played with a different endings on the second time.

Tiger Rag

1 & 2 & 3 & 4 &

1 & 2 & 3 & 4 &   1 & 2 & 3 & 4 &

Note C# (D♭)

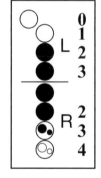  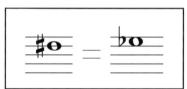

Remember: _ENHARMONIC NOTES_ - two notes that sound the same but are written differently.

Note D# (E♭)

Note E

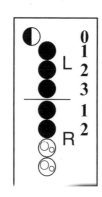

Play E

Tu   tu tu tu   tu   tu tu tu tu tu   tu tu   tu tu tu

Practice playing high notes (E-F-G). Tighten your lips slightly and blow a little harder than usual. Cover 2/3 to 3/4 of the thumb hole using the tip of your thumb. Or you could say uncover 1/3 to 1/4 of that opening. A little more than half of the hole remains covered.

Practice playing E - E' (E'- second octave E, i. e., higher by an octave). Find a steady sound and remember the feeling, your thumb opens a small slot for a slightly higher pitch.

Note F

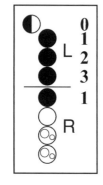

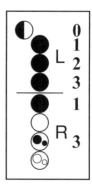

Baroque fingering system

Play F

Tu   tu   tu   tu   tu   tu   tu   tu   tu tu tu
1   &   2   &   1   &   2   &   1   &   2   &   1   &   2   &

Staccato

Dots placed above or below note heads indicate that the notes should be played staccato, in a detached manner. Musicians often play a staccato quarter note as if it were an eighth note followed by an eighth rest.

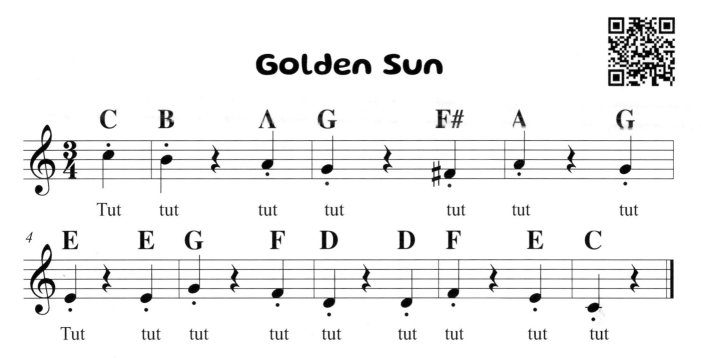

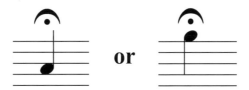

Fermata

A fermata can be found above a note or a rest. It simply means holding out the note for as long as you want to. It is the composer's idea to hold it for some type of length of time. If you specify the sounding time of a note under the fermats, then we can assume that the note (or pause) should be extended by the value of the original value, that is, twice as long. So, if it's a half note, then it sounds like a whole note. If a whole note, then it sounds like two whole notes, etc.

Fingering Chart (German system)

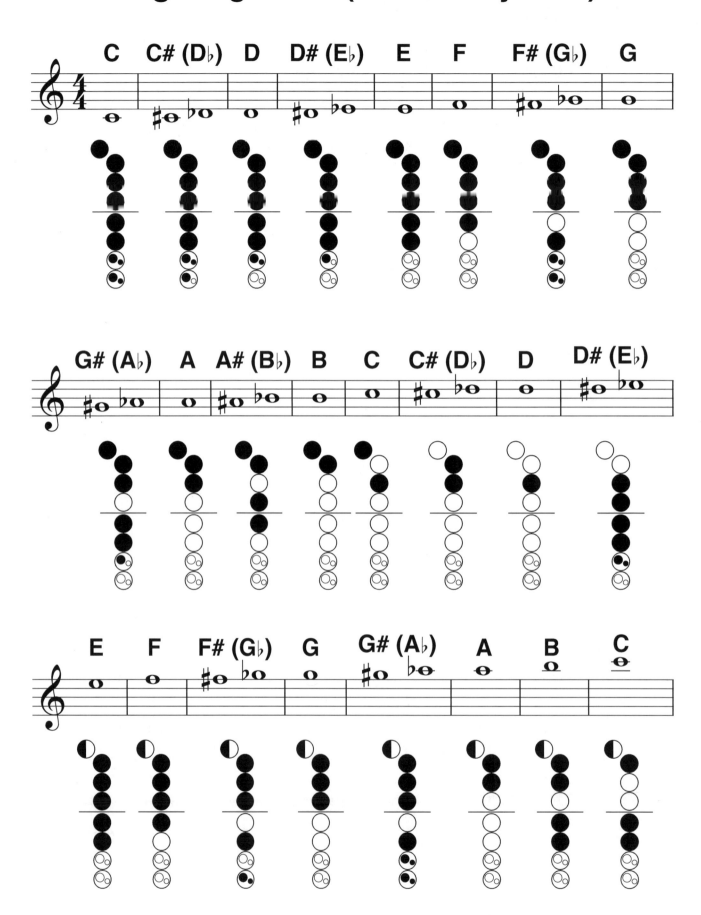

Baroque fingering system

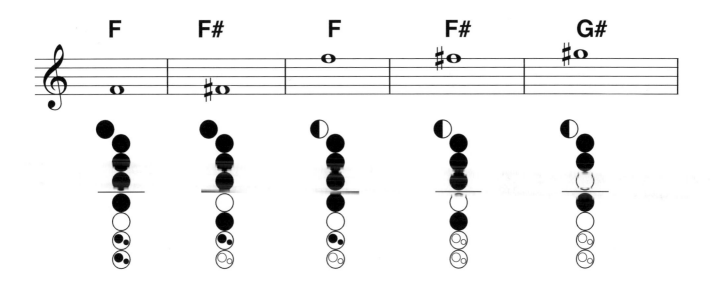

You can download the PDF via a direct link (for convenience):

cutt.ly/B8b0M4Q

or scan the QR code:

The most frequently played notes (German system)

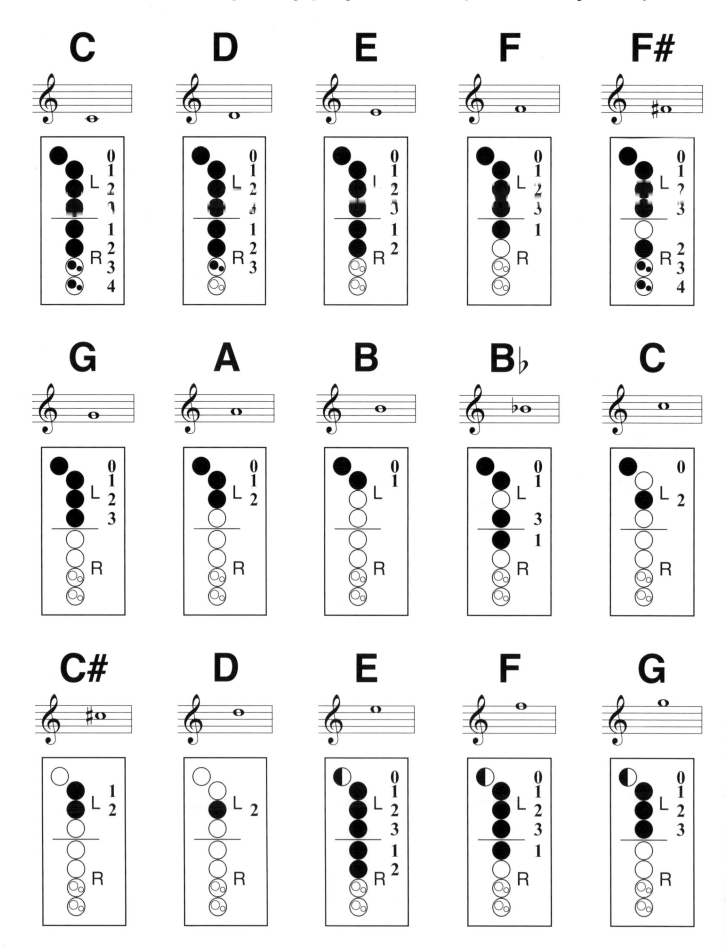

* You can download the PDF on p. 63

Chapter 3

ALL VIDEOS (Playlist)

All videos are also in the same playlist on YouTube:

or link:

cutt.ly/d8dN7YP

Messages about typos, errors, inaccuracies and suggestions for
improving the quality are gratefully received at:
avgustaudartseva@gmail.com

1. Little Sally Water

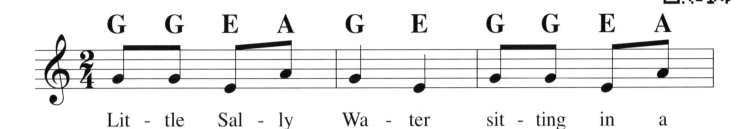

Lit - tle Sal - ly Wa - ter sit - ting in a

sau - cer, Rise Sal - ly, rise Sal - ly,

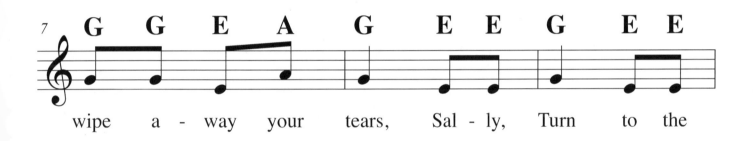

wipe a - way your tears, Sal - ly, Turn to the

east, Sal - ly, Turn to the west, Sal - ly Turn to the

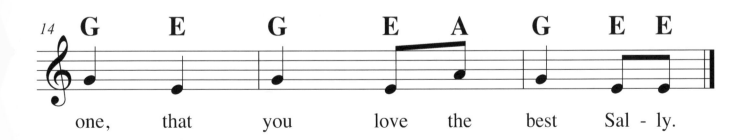

one, that you love the best Sal - ly.

2. O When The Saints

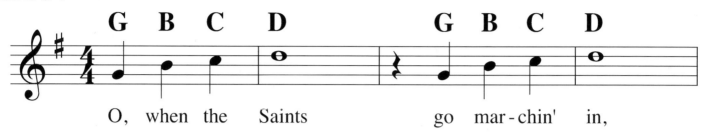

O, when the Saints go mar-chin' in,

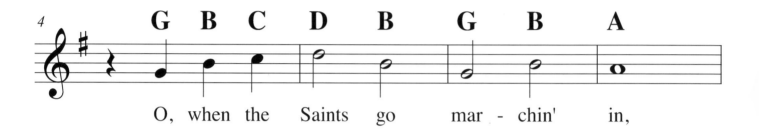

O, when the Saints go mar - chin' in,

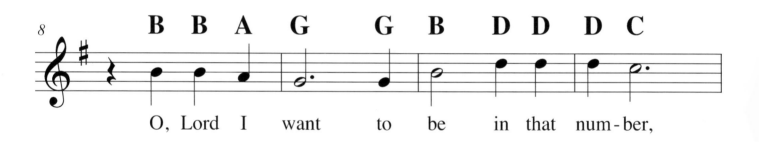

O, Lord I want to be in that num-ber,

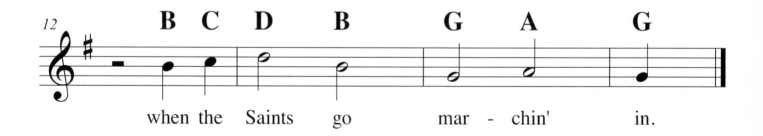

when the Saints go mar - chin' in.

3. Good Night, Ladies

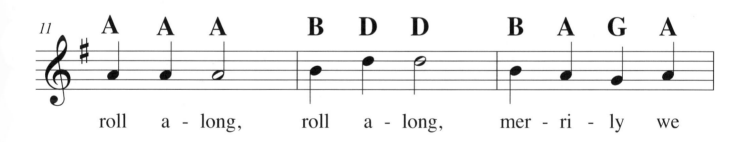

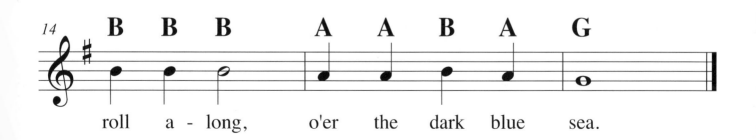

4. Hush Little Baby

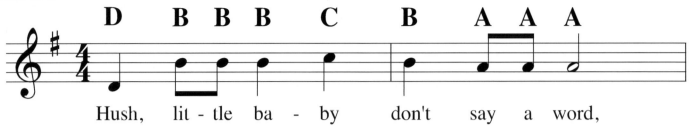

Hush, lit-tle ba - by don't say a word,

Pa - pa's gon - na buy you a mock - ing bird.

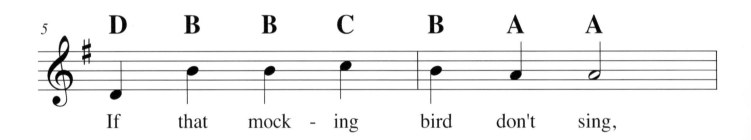

If that mock - ing bird don't sing,

Pa - pa's gon - na buy you a dia - mond ring.

5. Old MacDonald

Old Mac-Don-ald had a farm, ee-eye, ee-eye, oh! And

on that farm he had a cow, ee - eye ee - eye

oh! With a moo moo here, and a moo moo there,

here a moo, there a moo, ev'-ry-where a moo moo. Old Mac-Don-ald

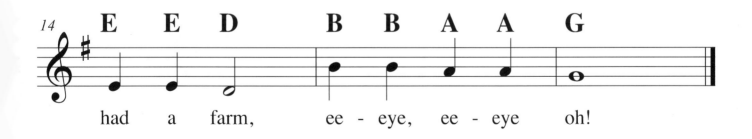

had a farm, ee - eye, ee - eye oh!

6. Jolly Old Saint Nicholas

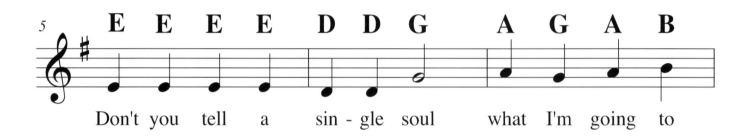

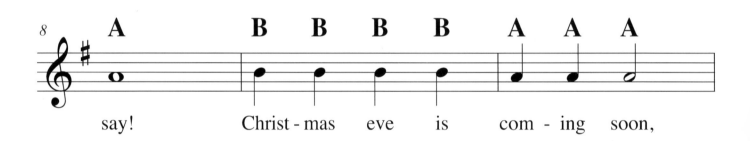

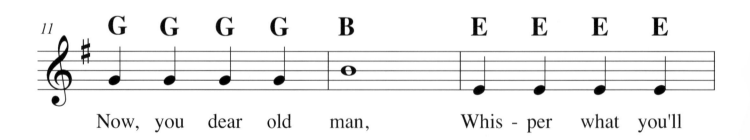

7. I've Got Peace Like A River

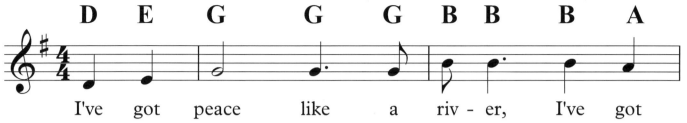

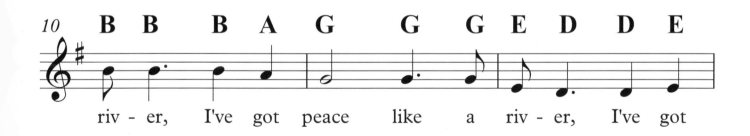

8. Amazing Grace

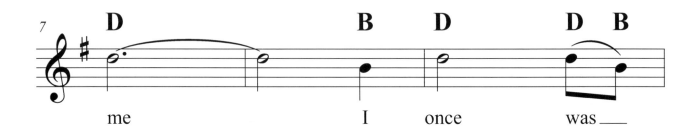

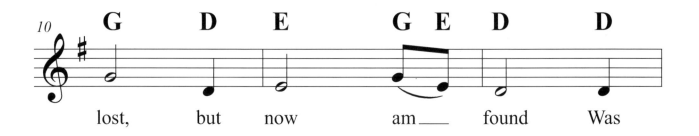

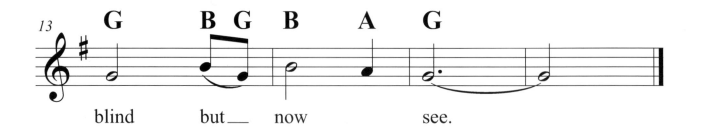

9. Silver Moon Boat

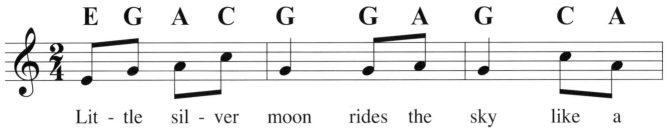

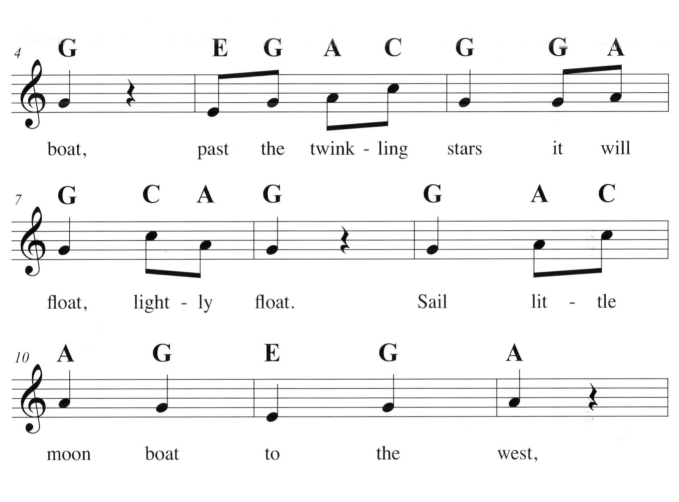

10. Hickory Dickory Dock

Hick - o - ry Dick - o - ry Dock,

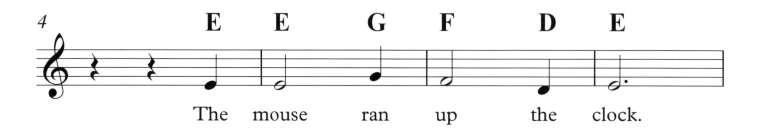

The mouse ran up the clock.

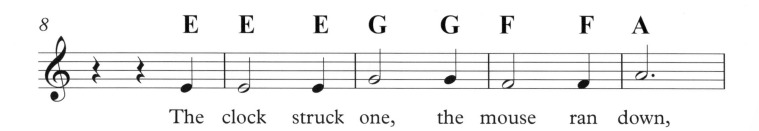

The clock struck one, the mouse ran down,

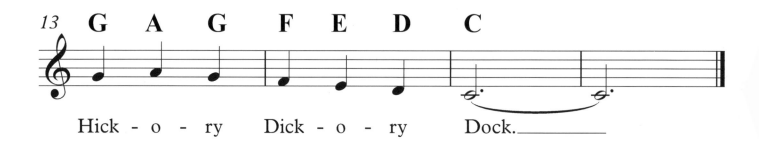

Hick - o - ry Dick - o - ry Dock._____

11. The Farmer In The Dell

The farm - er in the dell, The farm - er in the

dell, Heigh ho, the Der - ry O! The

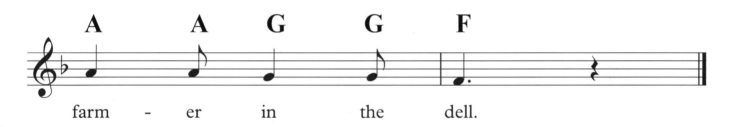

farm - er in the dell.

2. The farmer takes the wife
The farmer takes the wife
Heigh ho, the Derry O!
The farmer takes the wife.

12. Ring Around The Rosie

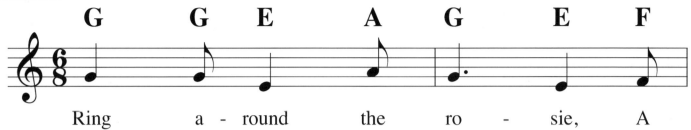

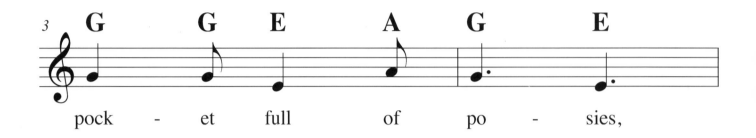

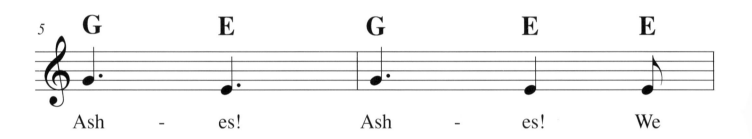

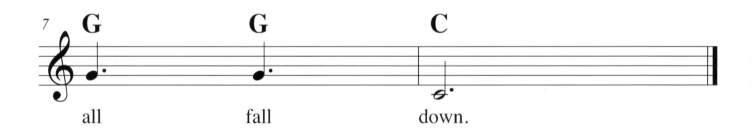

13. Billy Boy

14. Twinkle Twinkle Little Star

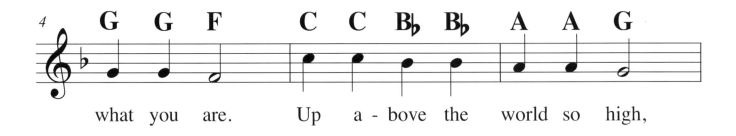

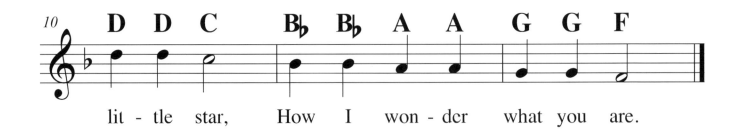

15. A-Tisket, A-Tasket

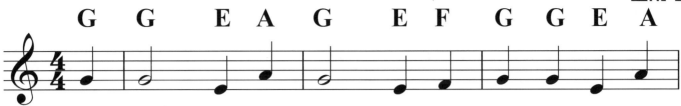

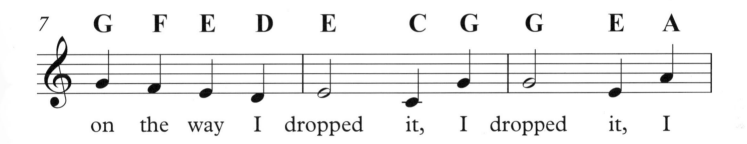

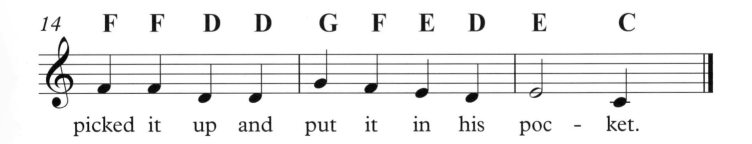

16. The Wheels On The Bus

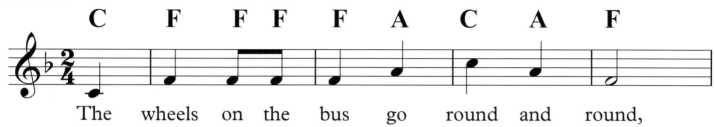

The wheels on the bus go round and round,

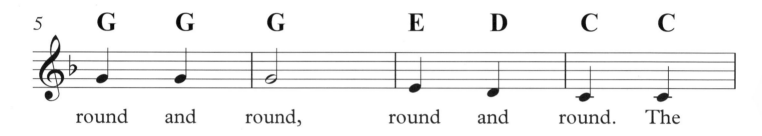

round and round, round and round. The

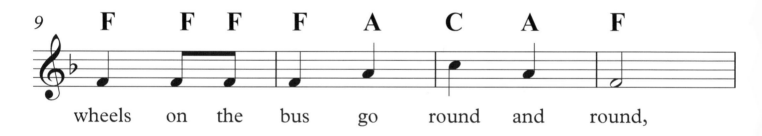

wheels on the bus go round and round,

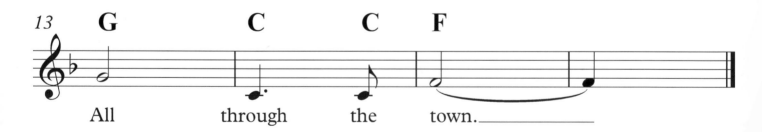

All through the town._____

17. London Bridge Is Falling Down

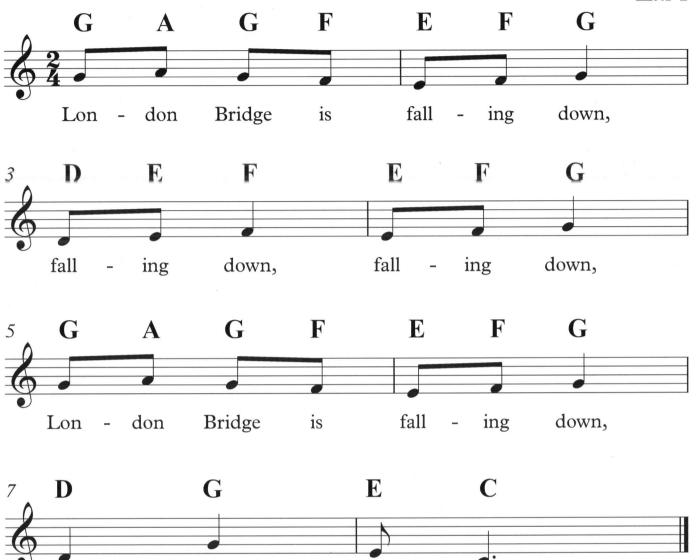

18. Baa, Baa, Black Sheep

19. Bingo

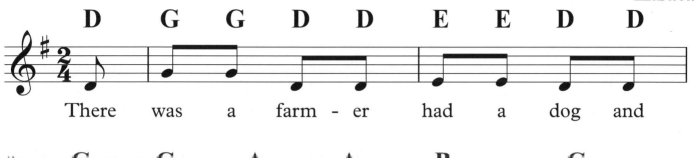

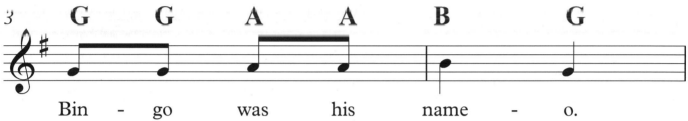

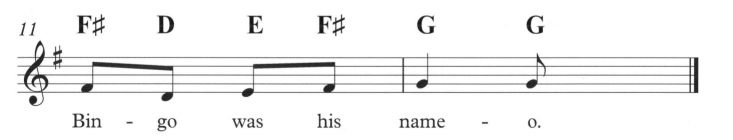

20. Skip To My Lou

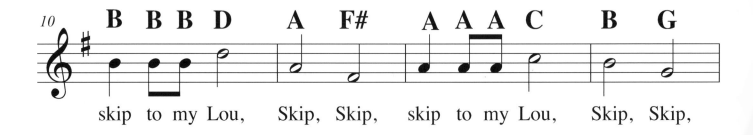

21. Clementine

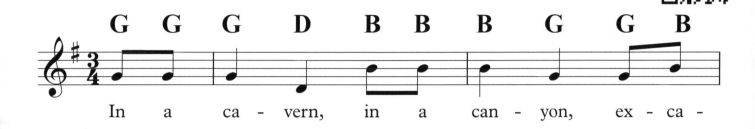

In a ca - vern, in a can - yon, ex - ca -

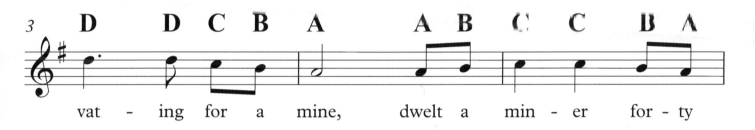

vat - ing for a mine, dwelt a min - er for - ty

nin - er, and his daugh - ter Cle - men - tine. Oh, my

dar - ling, Oh, my dar - ling, Oh, my dar - ling Cle - men -

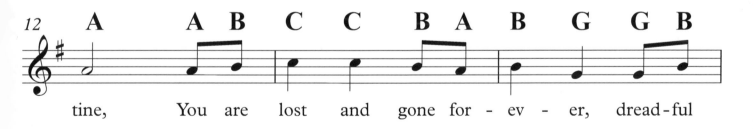

tine, You are lost and gone for - ev - er, dread - ful

sor - ry Cle - men - tine.

22. Scarborough Fair

23. Father Grumble

There was an old man that lived in a wood. As

you can plain-ly see, Who said he could do more

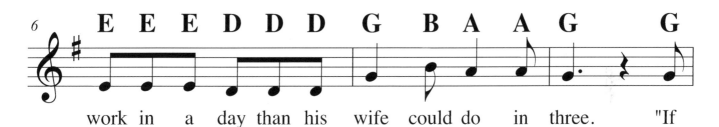

work in a day than his wife could do in three. "If

that be so," the old wo-man said, "Why this you must al-

low, That you shall do my work for a day while

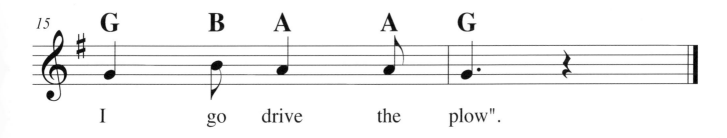

I go drive the plow".

24. Jennie Jenkins

Will you wear white, Oh my dear, Oh my dear?

Will you wear white, Jen - nie Jen - kins? No, I

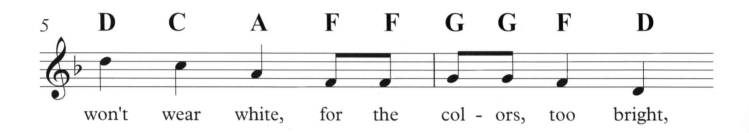

won't wear white, for the col - ors, too bright,

I'll___ buy me a fol - de - rol - dy, til - de - tol - dy, seek - a - dou - ble,

use - a - cause - a, roll - a - find - me, roll,_____ Jen - nie Jen - kins, roll.

25. Old Dan Tucker

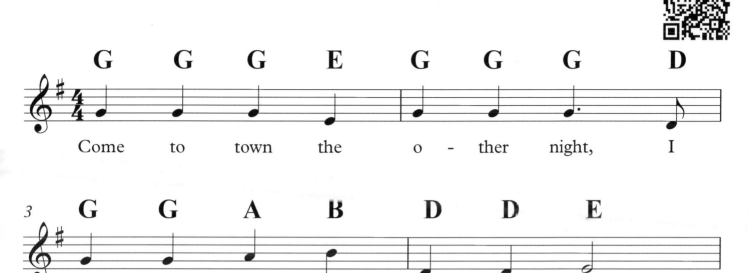

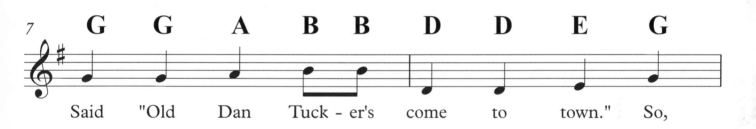

26. This Old Man

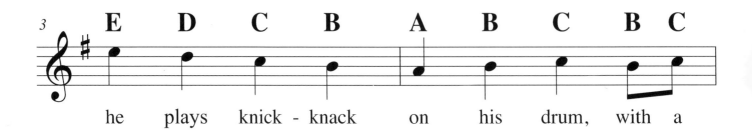

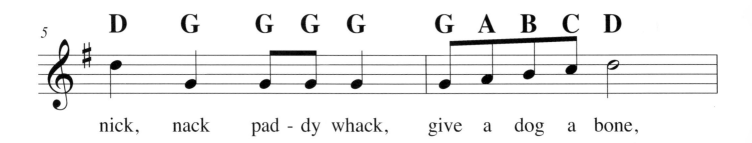

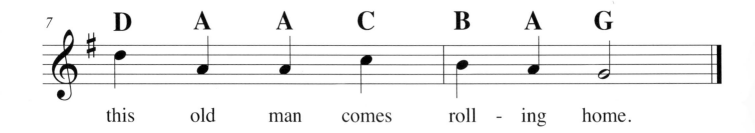

27. Lovely Evening

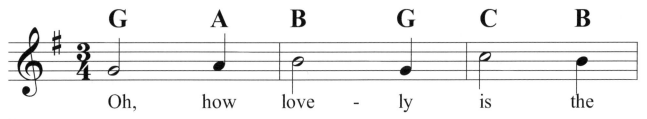

Oh, how love - ly is the

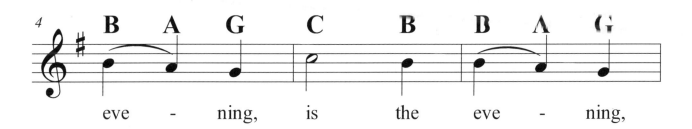

eve - ning, is the eve - ning,

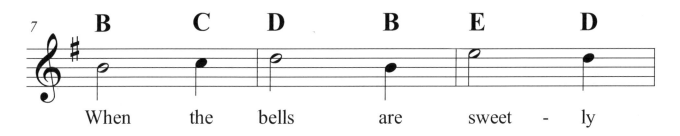

When the bells are sweet - ly

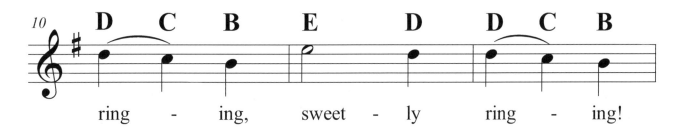

ring - ing, sweet - ly ring - ing!

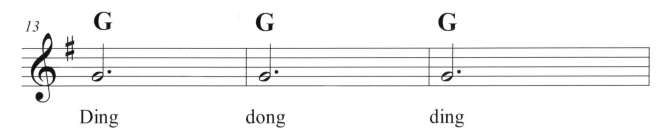

Ding dong ding

dong ding dong.

28. Joy To The World

Joy to the world! The Lord is come; Let

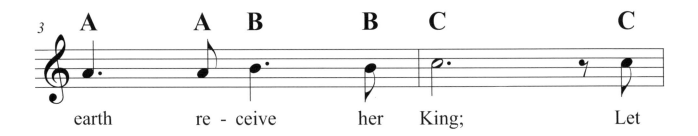

earth re - ceive her King; Let

ev - 'ry — he - art pre - pa - re Him ro - om. And

heaven and na - tu - re sing. And heaven and na - tu - re sing. And

heaven and hea - ven and na - ture sing.

29. Pop! Goes The Weasel

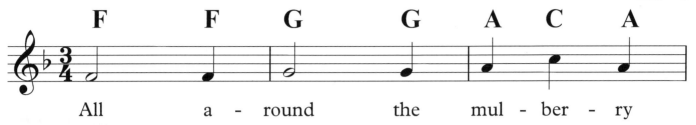

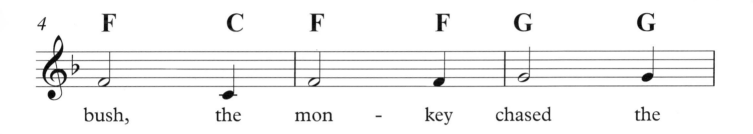

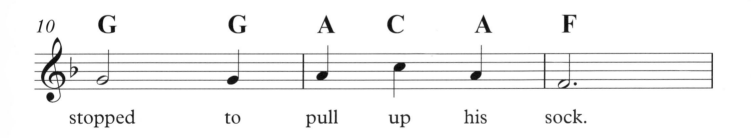

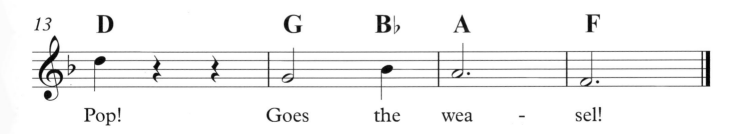

30. If You're Happy And You Know It

If you're hap-py and you know it clap your hands. If you're

hap - py and you know it clap your hands. If you're

hap-py and you know it, then your face will sure-ly show it, If you're

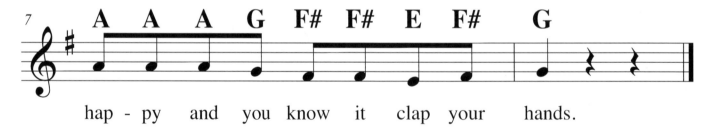

hap - py and you know it clap your hands.

96

31. Muffin Man

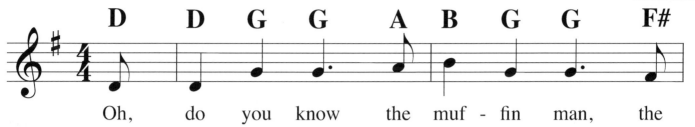

Oh, do you know the muf - fin man, the

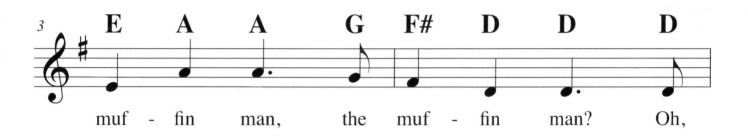

muf - fin man, the muf - fin man? Oh,

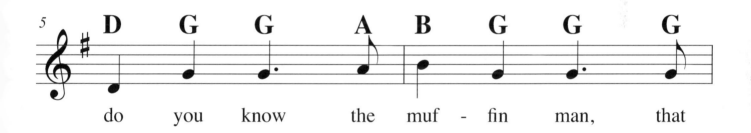

do you know the muf - fin man, that

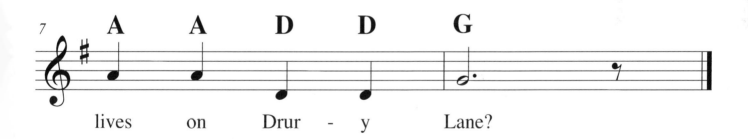

lives on Drur - y Lane?

32. This Land Is Your Land

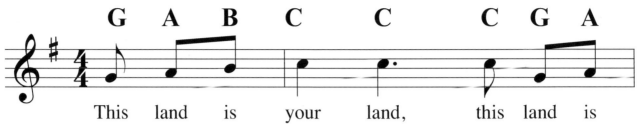

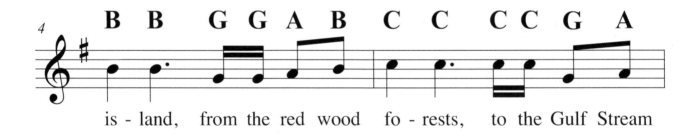

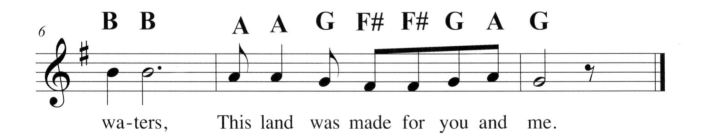

33. Ten Little Indians

One lit - tle, two lit - tle, three lit - tle In - di - ans

four lit - tle, five lit - tle, six lit - tle In - di - ans

se - ven lit - tle, eight lit - tle, nine lit - tle, In - di - ans,

ten lit - tle In - di - ans boys.

2. Ten little, nine little, eight little Indians,
Seven little, six little, five little Indians,
Four little, three little, two little Indians,
One little Indian boy.

34. Head, Shoulders, Knees And Toes

35. The North Wind Doth Blow

The north wind doth blow And we shall have snow And

what will poor rob - in do then? Poor thing! He'll

sit in the barn and keep him - self warm and

hide his head un - der his wing Poor thing!

36. Silent Night

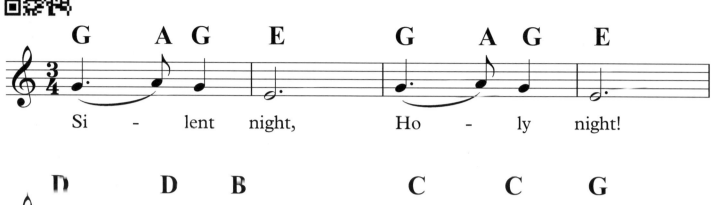

G A G E G A G E

Si - lent night, Ho - ly night!

D D B C C G

All is calm, all is bright.

A A C B A G A G E

Round yon Vir - gin, Moth - er and Child.

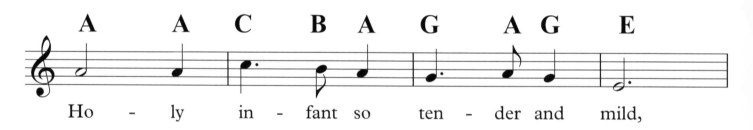

A A C B A G A G E

Ho - ly in - fant so ten - der and mild,

D D F D B C E

Sleep in heav - en - ly peace,_____

C G E G F D C

Sle - ep in heav - sen - ly peace._____

37. O Christmas Tree

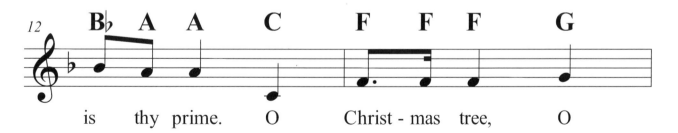

38. The First Noel

39. Away In A Manger

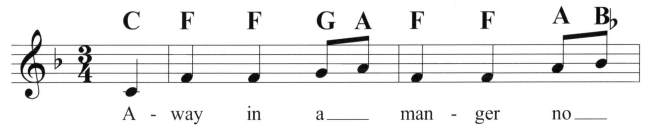

C F F G A F F A B♭

A - way   in   a ___ man - ger   no ___

C C D B♭ G A B♭ B♭ C

crib   for   a   bed,   the ___ lit - tle   Lord

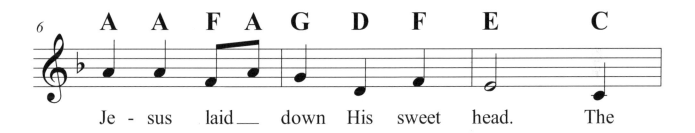

A A F A G D F E C

Je - sus   laid ___ down   His   sweet   head.   The

F F G A F F A B♭

stars   in   the ___ bright   sky   looked ___

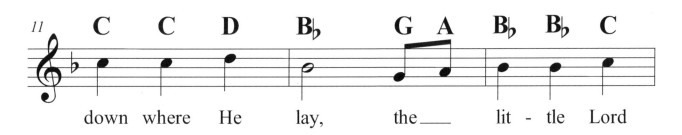

C C D B♭ G A B♭ B♭ C

down   where   He   lay,   the ___ lit - tle   Lord

A A F A G D E F

Je - sus   a - sleep   on   the   hay.

40. We Wish You A Merry Christmas

D G G A G F# E E E A A B A G

We wish you a mer-ry Christ-mas, we wish you a mer-ry

F# D D B B C B A G E D D E A F#

Christ-mas we wish you a mer-ry Christ-mas and a hap-py New

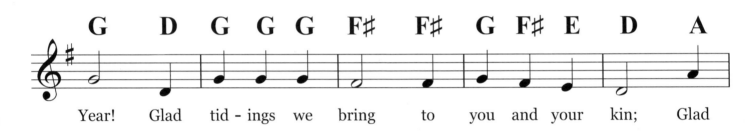

G D G G G F# F# G F# E D A

Year! Glad tid-ings we bring to you and your kin; Glad

B A G D D D D E A F# G D

tid-ings for Christ-mas and a hap-pay New Year! We

G G A G F# E E E A A B A G F# D D

wish you a mer-ry Christ-mas, we wish you a mer-ry Christ-mas, we

B B C B A G E D D E A F# G

wish you a mer-ry Christ-mas and a hap-py New Year!

41. Jingle Bells

42. Simple Gifts

'Tis the gift to be sim-ple, 'tis the gift to be free, 'Tis the

gift to come down where we ought to be, And when we find our-selves in the

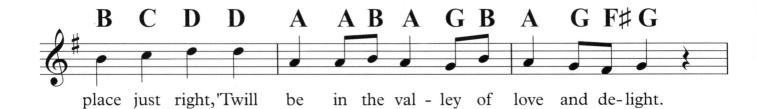

place just right, 'Twill be in the val - ley of love and de - light.

When true sim - plic - i - ty is gain'd, to bow and to bend we will

not be a-sham'd, to turn, turn will be our de-light, 'Till by

turn - ing, turn - ing we come 'round right.

43. Aura Lee

As the black-bird in the spring 'neath the wil-low

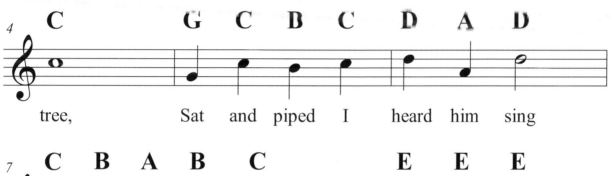

tree, Sat and piped I heard him sing

praising Au - ra Lee. Au - ra Lee!

Au - ra Lee! Maid of gold - en hair.

Sun - shine came a - long with thee and

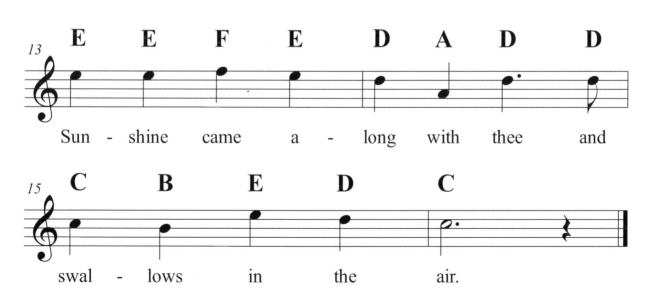

swal - lows in the air.

44. Buffalo Gals

45. All Through The Night

G F# E G A G F# D E F# F#

Sleep, my child and peace at-tend thee All through the

G G F# E G A G F# D

night; Guard - ian an - gels, God will send thee,

E F# F# G C B C D E D C B

All through the night. Soft and drow-sy hours are creep-ing,

C B A G B A G F# G F# E G

Hill and vale in slum-ber sleep-ing, Love a - lone his

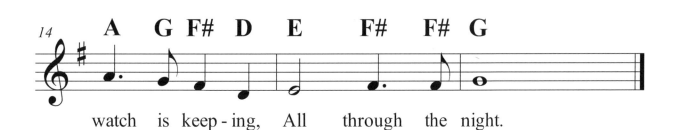

A G F# D E F# F# G

watch is keep - ing, All through the night.

46. Humpty Dumpty

Hump - ty Dump - ty sat on a wall.

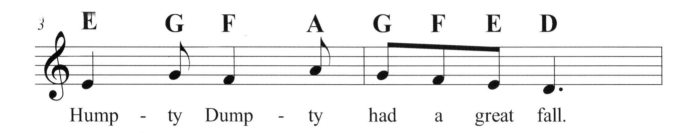

Hump - ty Dump - ty had a great fall.

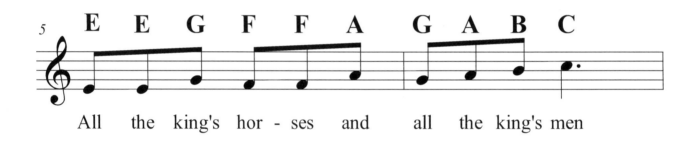

All the king's hor - ses and all the king's men

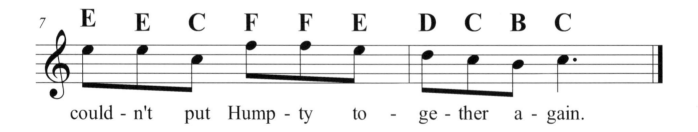

could - n't put Hump - ty to - ge - ther a - gain.

47. America The Beautiful

48. All The Pretty Little Horses

Hush-a-bye, don't you cry, go to sleep, my lit-tle

ba - by. When you wake, you shall have

all the pret-ty lit-tle hor - ses. Blacks and bays,

dap-ples and greys, Coach and six a lit-tle hor - ses.

Hush-a-bye, don't you cry, go to sleep my lit-tle ba - by.

49. America

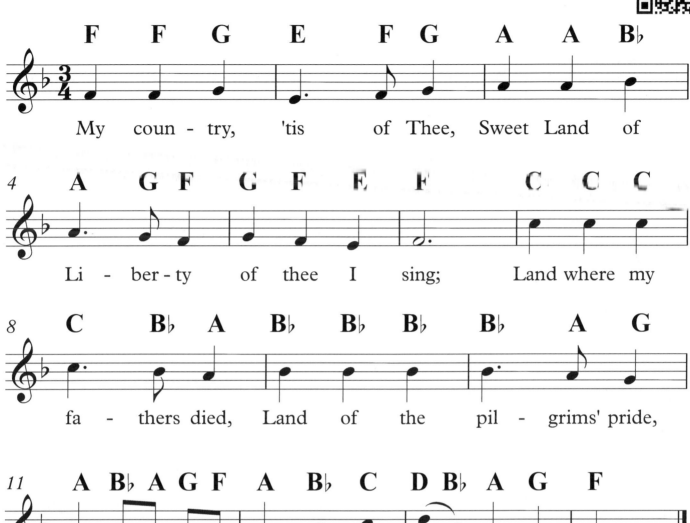

50. Keemo Kymo

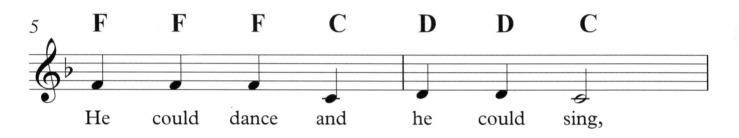

51. Oh, Dear! What Can The Matter Be?

G G G E C G E C F F F D E F E D

Oh, dear! What can the mat-ter be? Oh, dear! What can the mat-ter be?

G G G E C G E C D E F E F D C

Oh, dear! What can the mat-ter be? John-ny's so long at the fair.___

G G E F G E F G E C G E C

He pro-mised to buy me a trin-ket to please me, And

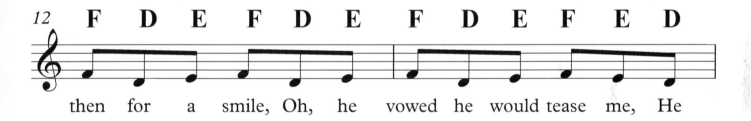

F D E F D E F D E F E D

then for a smile, Oh, he vowed he would tease me, He

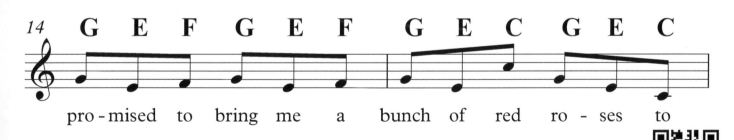

G E F G E F G E C G E C

pro-mised to bring me a bunch of red ro-ses to

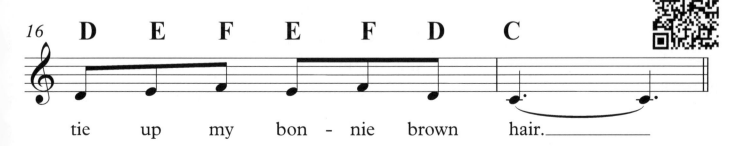

D E F E F D C

tie up my bon-nie brown hair.___

117

52. She'll Be Coming 'Round The Mountain

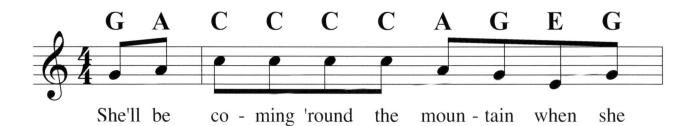

She'll be co - ming 'round the moun - tain when she

comes, She'll be co - ming 'round the moun - tain when she

comes, She'll be co - ming 'round the moun - tain, She'll be

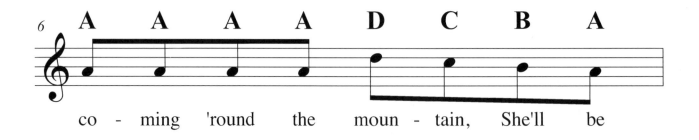

co - ming 'round the moun - tain, She'll be

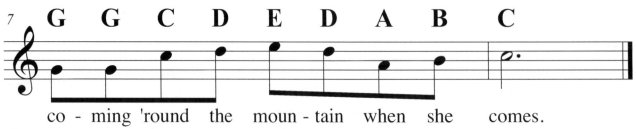

co - ming 'round the moun - tain when she comes.

53. Long, Long Ago

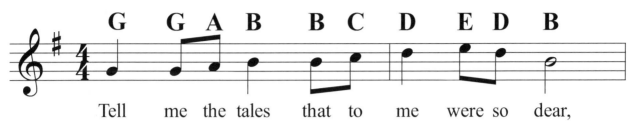

Tell me the tales that to me were so dear,

Long, long a-go, long, long a-go, Sing me the songs I de-

light-ed to hear, Long, long a-go, long a-go.

Now you are come all my grief is re-moved,

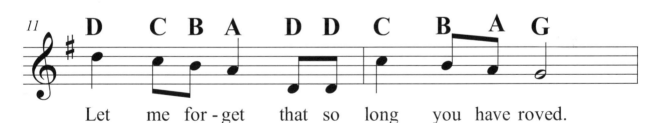

Let me for-get that so long you have roved.

Let me be-lieve that you love as you loved,

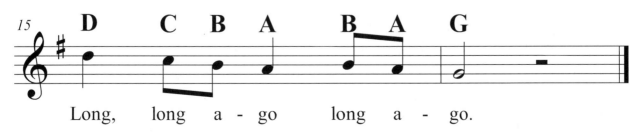

Long, long a-go long a-go.

54. Vacation Days

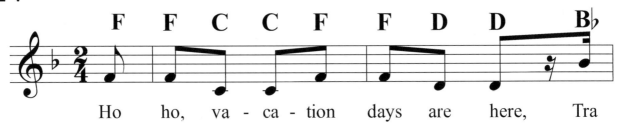

55. Little Brown Jug

G E G G G F A A A A

My wife and I lived all a-lone In a

B B B A B C D E F G G G

lit-tle log hut we called our own; She loved gin, and

F A A A B B A B C G C

I loved rum; I tell you what, we'd lots of fun.

G G G A A A B B B A B

Ha, ha, ha, you and me, "Lit-tle brown jug,"don't

C D E G G G A A A

I love thee; Ha, ha, ha, you and me

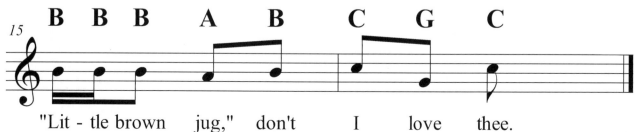

B B B A B C G C

"Lit - tle brown jug," don't I love thee.

56. Greensleeves

57. Wedding March

59. Auld Lang Syne

Should auld ac-quain-tance be for-got, and

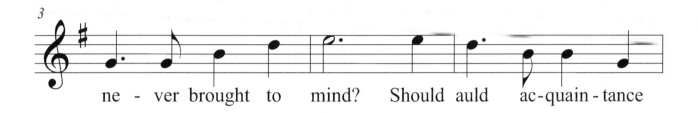

ne - ver brought to mind? Should auld ac-quain-tance

be for-got, and days of auld lang syne? For

auld___ lang___ syne, my jo, for auld___ lang___

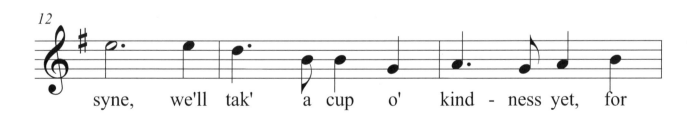

syne, we'll tak' a cup o' kind - ness yet, for

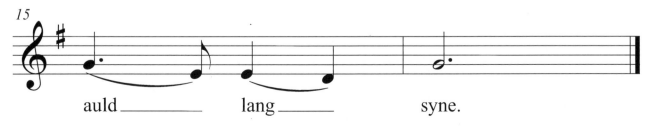

auld_____ lang_____ syne.

60. Oh! Susanna

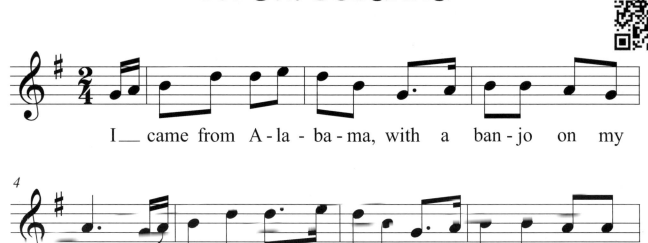

I came from A-la-ba-ma, with a ban-jo on my

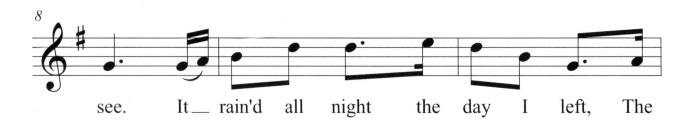

knee. I'm goin' to Loui-si-a-na, My true love for to

see. It rain'd all night the day I left, The

wea-ther it was dry. The sun so hot I froze to death, Su-

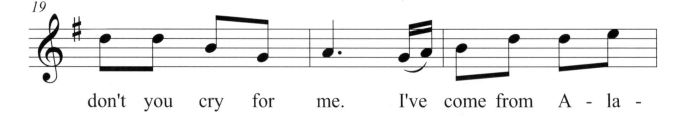

san-na don't you cry. Oh! Su-san-na, Oh

don't you cry for me. I've come from A-la-

126

ba-ma, with my ban-jo on my knee.

Made in the USA
Columbia, SC
25 August 2024